D1445883

CHILDREN OF POVERTY

STUDIES ON THE EFFECTS
OF SINGLE PARENTHOOD,
THE FEMINIZATION OF POVERTY,
AND HOMELESSNESS

edited by

STUART BRUCHEY
ALLAN NEVINS PROFESSOR EMERITUS
COLUMBIA UNIVERSITY

A GARLAND SERIES

AFRICAN AMERICAN CHILDREN WHO HAVE EXPERIENCED HOMELESSNESS

RISK, VULNERABILITY, AND RESILIANCE

NANCY C. COMPTON

GARLAND PUBLISHING, INC.
A MEMBER OF THE TAYLOR & FRANCIS GROUP
NEW YORK & LONDON / 1998

Library of Congress Cataloging-in-Publication Data

Compton, Nancy C., 1957–
    African American children who have experienced
homelessness : risk, vulnerability, and resiliance / Nancy C.
Compton.
        p.   cm. — (Children of poverty)
    Includes bibliographical references and index.
    ISBN 0-8153-3232-7 (alk. paper)
    1. Homeless children—United States—Psychology. 2. Afro-
American children—Psychology. 3. Homeless children—Services
for—United States.   I. Title.   II. Series.
HV4505.C66 1998
362.7'089'96073—dc21

                                                    98-42315

Printed on acid-free, 250-year-life paper
Manufactured in the United States of America

This book is dedicated to my mother
and to the women and children who took part in this study

Contents

Tables

Preface

While there are ever-increasing numbers of families with young children becoming homeless, little is known about interventions which can promote homeless childrens' resiliency. This study identifies factors that contribute to homeless children's positive outcomes. Seventeen African-American children and their mothers were identified through an agency that serves high-risk homeless families. The children were between the ages of three and six-and-a-half. Mothers' scores on the Center for Epidemiologic Studies Depression Scale (CES-D), the Taylor Manifest Anxiety Scale (TMAS), and twelve clusters of variables believed to be associated with children's functioning were compared for children who scored in the competent range on the Wechsler Preschool and Primary Scale of Intelligence-Revised (WPPSI-R) and on the Child Behavior Checklist (CBCL). Children's drawings and an observational measure developed by the researcher also were utilized.

Factors significantly associated with children's cognitive competency included: the mother's age at the time of her first birth; whether the child had attended Head Start or regular school; and the child's health status at birth. Mothers who started prenatal care earlier and who did not use drugs during their pregnancies delivered children who were more cognitively competent.

Children's resilient emotional/behavioral functioning was associated with their mothers' current psychological functioning and the amount of agency support they received. Children had significantly poorer outcomes if their mothers had been victims of a violent crime or battered by a partner during the preceding year.

While an encouraging finding was that the mean Full Scale IQ level of these children was in the Average range, a disturbing finding was the extent of emotional and behavioral disturbance in both the mothers and the children. The children drew pictures and told stories, as well as giving other verbal responses, which indicated that they had sustained significant psychological trauma. In the behavioral domain, girls were rated by their mothers as functioning significantly worse than boys, exhibiting a number of aggressive and destructive behaviors.

The results of this study can be used to inform public policy and are designed to be useful to any professionals who work with mothers and young children who have a history of homelessness.

Acknowledgments

A number of individuals contributed toward making this study possible and made significant contributions as it evolved. First of all, my deep appreciation is extended to Valata Jenkins-Monroe whose expertise in the area of African American families and the guidance she provided me from beginning to end added a great deal to this study. I am also grateful to Susan M. Greene for her critical reading, insights and support and G.G. Greenhouse, Director of Alameda County Health Care for the Homeless Program for her extensive knowledge about homeless families.

I am deeply indebted to The Better Homes Fund for their support, guidance and expertise on issues facing homeless families. I was fortunate to have worked closely with Bonnie Hausman who was associate director at that time, and have greatly benefited from the many publications of Ellen L. Bassuk, Angela Browne and Linda Weinreb.

My collaborative relationship with several staff who work on a daily basis with homeless families, and who shared their many experiences and insights added a great deal of richness both to my work and to this study. Special thanks to Kimi Watkins-Tartt, Ricky Pierre, Jeffrey Brown, Kimberly Jinnett, and Julie Tennant.

Throughout the process of writing this book I was fortunate to have the support of several friends, in particular, Andrea Gunderson, Debra Condren, Janet Ranney, Beth Krackov and Kathryn Orifer.

Two outstanding supervisors at the University of California, San Francisco, Alicia F. Lieberman, Director of the Child Trauma Research Project and Jeree H. Pawl, Director of the Infant-Parent Program have been and continue to be inspiring mentors in my life.

Acknowledgments

African American Children Who Have Experienced Homelessness

CHAPTER I

Introduction

STATEMENT OF THE PROBLEM

Families are the fastest-growing segment of the homeless population. Increasing numbers of women and children have joined the ranks of the homeless and are faring less and less well due to shifts in public policy and changing social mores. While estimates vary considerably as to the number of homeless children, it is widely agreed that youngest children are over-represented in the new wave of homeless (Bassuk, Rubin, & Lauriat, 1986; Institute of Medicine, 1988; Rog, Holupka & McCombs-Thorton, 1995).

Many women have become homeless due to issues related to what has been termed the "feminization of poverty," whereby divorce, desertion, and victimization leave women particularly vulnerable to falling through social safety nets. Because of the uneven distribution of resources and opportunities among the population, the burden of poverty falls disproportionately on African-American women and their children. This group is significantly over-represented among poor and homeless families (Bassuk & Rosenberg, 1988; Belle, 1982; D'Ercole & Struening, 1990; McChesney, 1991; Rog et al., 1995; Shinn, Knickman, & Weitzman, 1991; Ziesemer, Marcoux & Marwell, 1994).

While there is limited information on the status of homeless children, it is widely contended that children living in poverty are exposed to significant environmental risks and stressors. They are not only subjected to successive negative life events, but are forced to endure chronic, oppressive, frustrating conditions, often on a long-term basis. This is particularly true for children of color (Duncan & Rodgers, 1988; McLoyd, 1990). These circumstances place children at significant risk for suffering from psychological, social, intellectual, and physical impairment.

GOALS OF THIS STUDY

This research study identifies factors that distinguish between (1) children who have survived multiproblem families and at least one episode of homelessness and who show emotional, behavioral, and intellectual competence and (2) children who appear maladjusted and/or are incapable of performing age-appropriate developmental tasks. By identifying protective factors that appear to have aided the competent children in their adaption, the researcher hopes that models of prevention and intervention can be constructed to assist other children assessed to be at risk.

To date, the research on homeless children has documented a high degree of psychological dysfunction and developmental delays. Yet, we know from high-risk samples that there are a certain number of children who defy the odds. Rutter (1979), who is one of the most prominent researchers in the area of resiliency, states, "Many children do not succumb to deprivation, and it is important that we determine why this is so and what it is that protects them from the hazards they face" (p. 70).

The aims of the present study are consistent with the field of resiliency, which is concerned with looking for factors or circumstances that appear protective to children reared in deprived, inappropriate, or traumatic environments. By focusing on children who have managed to cope, the researcher aimed to identify why some children appear resilient and others give up and lose hope when faced with the same adversities.

RESEARCH QUESTIONS

1. To what extent is the mother's resilient status, as measured by her current level of psychological distress, obtained level of academic and occupational competency, and past history of psychological coping, associated with her child's emotional/behavioral competency?

2. To what extent are mothers' stressful life events, particularly those that limit their availability to their children, associated with the children's emotional/behavioral resiliency?

3. To what extent does a family's degree of economic hardship predict children's emotional/behavioral and cognitive status?

4. To what extent do the number of supportive resources available to a family impact on the children's emotional/behavioral functioning and cognitive competency?

5. To what extent is children's cognitive and emotional/behavioral functioning effected by birth/health status, stressful life events, the number of children in the family, and their ordinal position?

Given these research questions, the principal objectives of this study are:

1. To identify the developmental status of young children who have experienced an episode of homelessness.

2. To identify the characteristics and life circumstances of competent/resilient children.

3. To identify the interrelationship between these children's developmental status and their birth and health history, their mothers' history of coping and current psychological functioning, their mothers' acquired competencies, the families' exposure to poverty and stressful life events, and the extent to which the families have been able to gain access to social support and resources.

4. To make recommendations for intervention services for children who have experienced an episode of homelessness.

In accordance with the ecological nature of this study, which emphasizes the interplay between individual, family, and environmental conditions, the literature review has been divided up into the following sections: (1) *Characteristics of the Child* (temperament, constitution, birth status, drug exposure, and gender); (2) *Mother-Child Variables* (availability, attunement, and attachment between mother and child); (3) *Risk Factors* (homeless status, poverty, single parenting, raising young children, family size/spacing, racial minority status, history of trauma, loss, and victimization in mother's life, and mother's current mental health status); and (4) *Protective Factors* (mother's resiliency: competency and coping behaviors and social support). Initial sections include: an overview of the problem of homelessness; a review of studies on the psychological and developmental status of homeless children; and a section that defines resiliency and summarizes the major studies that have been done in the area.

CHAPTER II

Literature Review

SCOPE OF THE PROBLEM

The prevalence of homeless families with children is difficult to ascertain for the following reasons: (1) there is no agreed-upon definition of the homeless; and (2) many families are not counted because they do not stay in conventional places like homeless shelters. While some organizations include in their numbers families that have been displaced from their homes and are living in tight quarters with other families, other organizations do not.

There is a consensus among researchers that families (mostly female-headed) are a rapidly growing population and are becoming a greater proportion of the entire homeless population. Most researchers report that families make up more than one-third of the entire homeless population (Melnick & Williams, 1987; Reyes & Waxman, 1989; U.S. Conference of Mayors, 1993).

Children are the fastest-growing group among the homeless. Estimates cited by the Children's Defense Fund (1991) range from 61,500 nightly (Urban Institute, 1988) to more than 500,000 annually (National Coalition for the Homeless, 1990). The majority of homeless children are under the age of six (Weinreb & Bassuk, 1990).

Based on soaring poverty rates, the rising number of homeless children is expected to get much worse rapidly. McChesney (1991) states, "All children whose families are living under the poverty line (and some who are not) are at risk of becoming homeless as long as there is a shortage of affordable low-income housing" (p. 144).

The number of children living in poverty increased by 2.2 million during the decade between 1979 and 1989 and currently stands at 21%

(Children's Defense Fund, 1991). Estimates are that 14.8 million children will live in poverty by the year 2000 (Children's Defense Fund, 1991). The rate of poverty for children is now the highest of any age group. One in five children (one in four preschoolers) is poor (Children's Defense Fund, 1991).

Children in female-headed families are five times more likely than children in other families to be poor. Minority children are significantly more likely to be poor than non-minority children (43.7% versus 14.8%, respectively) and remain poor for substantially longer periods of time. The rate of poverty among African-American high school dropouts is an astronomical 93.4% (Children's Defense Fund, 1991).

The causes of homelessness are many. Melnick and Williams (1987) attribute the problem to an "interconnectiveness between societal neglect and personal misfortune" (p. 4). The majority of homeless become so due to environmental forces beyond their control and over which they have little responsibility.

The largest reason for the soaring numbers of homeless is the decline in affordable low-income housing. Some of the precipitating factors that can contribute to families becoming displaced include: lost, reduced, or insufficient benefits; low wages; inadequate or no child support; and unemployment. As welfare programs tighten their eligibility requirements and cut funds, housing is taking a significantly larger proportion of low-income families' benefits. Oftentimes, poor mothers cannot turn to other network members for assistance because their friends and families are just as financially strapped as they are.

Other circumstances that lead to homelessness include: disasters such as fires or earthquakes; prejudice and related societal barriers; family violence; and pregnancy. Certain vulnerable groups have been identified in the literature. These include women from multiproblem families who have suffered childhood abuse and/or losses at a young age; women who have been victimized in adulthood; women who have drug abuse or mental health problems; and women who have inadequate social support systems.

Milburn and D'Ercole (1991) reviewed research which showed that "most homeless women are mothers, are under 35 years of age, are members of a minority group, have often not completed high school, and have usually experienced more than one episode of homelessness in their lifetimes" (p. 1161).

Rog, Holupka and McCombs-Thornton (1995) reported from their large scale evaluation program for homeless families across nine metropolitan sites the following demographic data: the majority of the families consisted of a single female parent who was approximately 30 years old with two children; nearly 60% had obtained a high school diploma or its equivalent; and 92% had previously been employed.

In Oakland, California, the Emergency Services Network (1990) reported that families comprised 66% of the homeless population in 1985 and 71% of the homeless population in 1989. A significant factor in Oakland is the high rate of crack-cocaine addiction, which has eroded family structures and been the root cause of disaffiliations between network members. Fragmented networks are no longer able to buffer individuals from homelessness as they have in the past.

Between 1985 and 1989, the percentage of emergency shelter residents in Oakland with drug and/or alcohol problems rose from 6% to 63% of the total shelter population (Emergency Services Network of Alameda County, 1990). Other contributing factors in Oakland include a loss in unskilled and entry-level jobs and the 1989 earthquake, which damaged and destroyed many low-income units.

STUDIES OF THE DEVELOPMENTAL AND PSYCHOLOGICAL STATUS OF HOMELESS CHILDREN

There is little empirical data on the cognitive, behavioral, and socioemotional functioning of homeless children. The studies that do exist vary in regard to their methodology—some having control groups and utilizing standardized tests, and others relying more on data of a descriptive nature.

One of the most comprehensive series of studies was conducted by Bassuk and her colleagues (Bassuk, 1986; Bassuk & Rosenberg, 1990; Bassuk & Rubin, 1987; Bassuk, Rubin, & Lauriat, 1986). They studied 156 homeless children, primarily under the age of six, from 82 families living in 14 different shelters in Massachusetts. They also reported on comparison analyses of the performance of homeless and poor housed children on a number of developmental and psychological inventories. In the section that follows, there is a summary of their research findings in addition to the results of other researchers who have interviewed, observed, and tested young homeless children.

Cognitive Functioning

Bassuk and her colleagues used the Denver Developmental Screening Test (DDST) to assess developmental status in the areas of gross and fine motor skills, language, and personal and social development. Bassuk, Rubin, and Lauriat (1986) reported that 47% of the children age five or younger whom they assessed had at least one developmental lag, 33% had two or more, and 14% failed in all four areas. Overall, 37% demonstrated language delays, 34% could not complete the personal and social developmental tasks, 18% lacked gross motor skills, and 15% lacked fine motor coordination.

When a subset of the homeless preschool sample (those sheltered in Boston) was compared with 75 low-income housed preschoolers, 54% of the shelter sample versus 16% of the housed poor sample exhibited at least one developmental delay. Sheltered children performed worse in every developmental area tested. In comparison, 42% versus 3% could not complete the personal and social development tasks, 42% versus 13% manifested language delays, 17% versus 4% lacked gross motor skills, and 15% versus 1% lacked fine motor coordination (Bassuk & Rosenberg, 1990). These results are particularly striking in light of the fact that the DDST has been reported to under-refer children who actually manifest developmental lags (Meisels, 1989).

Wagner and Menke (1990) reported results similar to the ones described above by Bassuk and her colleagues. They also utilized the DDST to assess 162 homeless children age five or younger in Ohio. In this sample, 44% of the children manifested at least one developmental delay, and 24% manifested two or more. When these numbers were broken down into particular areas, 23% manifested language delays, 12% could not complete the personal and social developmental tasks, and 17% lacked gross motor skills. One of the most striking findings was that 30% of the assessed children lacked fine motor coordination.

However, other studies utilizing the DDST with homeless children did not report such discrepant findings. Lewis and Meyers (1989), for instance, reported that of the 212 homeless children under the age of six who were evaluated by nurse practitioners, only 5% had questionable or identified developmental lags, a rate that does not exceed that which one would expect to find in the general population.

Wood, Valdez, Hayashi, and Shen (1990) also utilized the DDST to study developmental delays in a sample of homeless Los Angeles preschoolers. They reported that 15% manifested at least one developmental delay, and 9% manifested two or more delays. This broke down into 13% manifesting a language delay, 11% lacking fine motor coordination, and 5% being unable to complete the personal-social development tasks.

Whitman and her colleagues (Whitman, 1987; Whitman, Accardo, Boyert, & Kendagor, 1990) assessed the cognitive and language abilities of 88 homeless children under the age of five living in a dormitory-style shelter in Missouri. Using the Peabody Picture Vocabulary Test-Revised (PPVT-R), they found that 67% manifested delays in their capacity to use and produce language. On the Slosson Intelligence Test, 35% scored at or below the borderline area on cognitive development.

Rescorla, Parker, and Stolley (1991) assessed 40 homeless children between the ages of three and five and compared them to a group of 20 housed children who were awaiting treatment at a pediatric clinic in Philadelphia. They found that shelter children were significantly more delayed in receptive vocabulary as measured by the PPVT-R and performed significantly less well on the Beery Developmental Test of Visual-Motor Integration.

Fox, Barrnett, Davies, and Bird (1990) assessed 4 to 10-year-old children who were staying at one of five New York City hotels that sheltered homeless families. Of the 49 children who completed the PPVT-R, 30 (61%) performed at the age-adjusted 1st percentile, reflecting significant deficits in receptive verbal functioning; 9 (18%) performed between the 2nd and 10th percentiles; 8 (16%) performed between the 10th and 34th percentiles; and only 2 (4%) scored between the 50th and 59th percentiles. In addition, 48 children (98%) completed the Visual-Motor Inventory. Of these, 19 (40%) scored below the 10th percentile, another 19 (40%) scored between the 10th and 35th percentiles, and only 10 children (20%) scored above the 35th percentile. These results show that the majority of children scored far below their age levels in cognitive ability as assessed by these tests.

Molnar and Rath (1990) used the Early Screening Inventory (ESI) to assess speech, language, cognition, perception, and gross and fine motor coordination in a sample of 84 homeless and 76 poor housed children between the ages of three and five in New York City. There were no significant differences in performance between the two groups, with both groups performing poorly. The only significant finding was that children who had received day-care services performed significantly better than those who had not.

Among school-aged children, Bassuk (1986) reported that 45% of a homeless sample of children had repeated at least one grade, and 25%

were in special classes. Similarly, Gewirtzman and Fodor (1987) reported that 54% of school-aged children had repeated a grade, and 29% had been placed in special education classes. Two-thirds of the elementary school aged students studied by Ziesemer and Marcoux (1994) were perceived by their teachers as performing below grade level. It is noteworthy that more than a quarter of the homeless children were perceived as functioning at or above grade level.

Donahue and Tuber (1995) reported a significant relationship for school-age homeless children between their level of aspiration and length of stay in homeless shelters. They state, "Children who do not live in a protective environment are not as likely to have achieved the sense of security and self-confidence necessary to develop and pursue challenging goals" (p.249). These authors conclude that "homelessness exerts its influence over time, limiting children's sense of accomplishment and curtailing their hopes for future success" (p.254).

Psychological Functioning

Several studies have reported that homeless children exhibit more anxiety, depression, and behavioral disturbances than housed and clinical populations of children (Bassuk & Rosenberg, 1988; Bassuk, Rubin, & Lauriat, 1986; Molnar & Rath, 1990; Rescorla, Parker & Stolley, 1991).

Bassuk, Rubin, and Lauriat (1986) assessed 44 homeless children over the age of five with the Children's Depression Inventory, a test that evaluates feelings of sadness during the previous two weeks. Fifty-four percent of the homeless children scored above the cutoff point of 9, indicating a need for psychiatric evaluation, and 31% were assessed to be clinically depressed. The mean score of 10.4 for the homeless sample was significantly higher than the mean score of 8.3 for the housed comparison group. In addition, the homeless children scored higher than six of the eight clinical comparison groups assessed during the development of the test. In a subsequent comparison of sheltered and housed poor children, Bassuk and Rosenberg (1990) reported that 52% of the sheltered and 48% of the housed sample scored in the clinical range as measured by the Children's Depression Inventory. There was no significant difference between the two groups.

Bassuk, Rubin, and Lauriat (1986) measured children over the age of five on the Children's Manifest Anxiety Scale. Of the 50 homeless children who completed the scale, 48% scored in the clinical range, indicating a need for psychiatric evaluation. In a subsequent comparison of housed versus sheltered children, 31% of the sheltered and 9% of the housed sample scored in the clinical range, yielding nonsignificant differences between the two groups in manifest anxiety (Bassuk & Rosenberg, 1990).

Bassuk and Rosenberg (1988) used the Simmons Behavior Checklist to assess behavioral problems of a sample of three to five-year-olds. They compared the homeless children to both a sample of nonclinical children and a sample of emotionally disturbed children. They reported that 55% of the homeless preschool children scored significantly higher than the other two samples. In comparison to the housed sample, the homeless children were reported by their mothers to have more sleep problems, shyness, inattention, delayed speech, aggression, and withdrawal. Homeless children scored significantly lower than both comparison groups in the area of being afraid of new things. When a later analysis was performed between 21 homeless and 33 housed poor children, no significant differences were found (Bassuk & Rosenberg, 1990).

A number of researchers have utilized the Achenbach Child Behavior Checklist (CBCL) to assess socioemotional functioning. The different research studies consistently report a high rate of disturbance in homeless children.

Rescorla, Parker, and Stolley (1991) used the CBCL to compare 40 homeless primarily African-American three to five-year-olds with a clinic sample of children and found that the homeless children had significantly more emotional/behavioral problems. The homeless children had significantly more difficulties of both an internalizing and externalizing nature suggesting a high level of depression and anxiety, in addition to aggression and destructiveness. As is typically the case in all populations of children, the girls displayed more internalizing symptoms, and the boys displayed more externalizing symptoms.

Molnar and Rath (1990), as cited in Rafferty and Shinn (1991), used the CBCL to compare 84 homeless and 76 poor housed children between the ages of three and five. Significantly more homeless children compared to the housed sample scored above the clinical cutoff—33% versus 11%, respectively.

Fox, Barrnett, Davies, and Bird (1990) reported that in their sample of 50 homeless children between the ages of four and ten who were being sheltered in New York City, 32% exhibited emotional and behavioral problems as assessed by parental report on the CBCL.

Vostanis, Grattan, Cumella and Winchester (1997) used the CBCL to compare 249 homeless children with a mean age of seven with a control group of low income housed children. Significantly more homeless children (28.4%) scored in the clinical range for internalizing or externalizing behaviors when compared with the housed controls (18.1%).

Molnar, Klein, Knitzer, and Ortiz-Torres (1988) reported on data collected by Bank Street College of Education teachers who were placed at 14 early childhood programs in New York City. The teachers observed two-and-a-half to five-year-old homeless children and noted the following characteristics: short attention spans, withdrawal, aggression, speech delays, sleep disorders, regressive toddler-like behaviors, inappropriate social interaction with adults, immature peer interaction, and immature motor behavior. These preschoolers had difficulty staying on task without one-on-one contact with an adult. The children were also observed to have a low threshold for frustration and displayed many attention-seeking behaviors. In contrast to their cool and distant interaction with their mothers, they exhibited indiscriminate contact with adult strangers and were unusually attached to their siblings.

The Citizen's Committee for Children (1988) reported from its study of 83 families sheltered in New York City that 66% of parents observed negative behavioral changes in their children since becoming homeless. Both acting-out and depressive symptoms were noted.

In summary, compared to housed poor children, homeless children tend to manifest a larger number of developmental delays. They also exhibit severe depression, a high degree of anxiety, and numerous behavior problems and learning difficulties. Despite these documented mental health problems and academic delays, few homeless children ever receive psychological treatment or special education services (Zima, Wells & Freeman, 1994).

DEFINING THE CONSTRUCT OF RESILIENCE

There is no agreed-upon definition or term to describe children who appear competent and resilient despite having been challenged with a significant amount of adversity. Competent children have been referred to by a variety of terms, such as: "invulnerable" (Anthony, 1974; Anthony & Cohler, 1987; Garmezy, 1971, 1974, 1976, 1981; Hetherington, 1984); "stress-resistant" (Garmezy, 1976, 1981, 1987;

Garmezy, Masten, & Tellegren, 1984); "resilient" (Block & Block, 1980; Hetherington, 1984; Rutter, 1979; Werner, 1984); "superkids" (Kauffman, Grunebaum, Cohler, & Garner, 1979; Pines, 1979); "invincible" (Werner & Smith, 1982); and "survivors" (Radke-Yarrow & Sherman, 1990). Others have relied on such terms as "coping" (Murphy & Moriarty, 1976); "hardiness" (Kobasa, 1979); and "ego-strength," "stress tolerance," "frustration tolerance," and "ego resilience" (Appley & Trumbull, 1967).

The popular label of "invulnerable," used extensively in the 1970s, has been avidly disputed on the grounds that it implies that there is a possibility of total psychological immunity. Rutter (1985), for example, did not believe that some children are so constitutionally tough that they will not succumb under the pressures of stress and adversity. He stated, "The resistance to stress is relative, not absolute; the bases of the resistance are both environmental and constitutional; and the degree of resistance is not a fixed quality—rather, it varies over time and according to circumstance" (p. 599). In his contact with people who had endured extremely stressful circumstances, Rutter (1979) also observed that the experiences had "usually left their mark" (p. 51).

Masten, Morison, Pellegrini, and Tellegen (1990) similarly state, "We surmise that there is no general 'immunity' to stress. Instead, there may be different patterns of stress responding that are more or less adaptive, depending on the context, the circumstances, and the developmental stage of the child" (p. 249). Anthony and Cohler (1987) stated their preference for the term "invulnerable" because "it seemed to us to make the point of psychological invincibility much more strikingly than the term resilience" (p. xi).

Murphy and Moriarty (1976) found no invulnerable children in their Coping Studies. They believe that when children are confronted with severe stress, there is always some degree of compromised functioning. They state that "few if any are so robust, so completely lacking in small as well as moderate or major handicaps as to be totally free from some zone of vulnerability. Most children have a checkerboard of strengths and weaknesses . . . , or a cluster of tendencies that interact in such a way as to produce one or another pattern of vulnerability as well as strength" (p. 202).

DEFINITIONS OF RESILIENCE

The way in which different researchers operationalize stress resistance varies significantly. Rutter (1981) describes resilient children as those "young people who 'do well,' in some sense, in spite of having experienced a form of 'stress' which in the population as a whole is known to carry a substantial risk of an adverse outcome" (pp. 323-324).

Waters and Sroufe (1983) define a competent individual as "one who is able to make use of environmental and personal resources to achieve a good developmental outcome" (p.81) while Grinker (1968) cites John Whitehorn as defining resilient individuals as those who "work well, play well, love well and expect well" p. 23.   Werner and Smith (1982) define resilience as children's "capacity to cope effectively with the internal stresses of their vulnerabilities (such as labile patterns of autonomic reactivity, developmental imbalances, unusual sensitivities) and external stresses (such as illness, major losses, and dissolution of the family)" (p. 4).

Radke-Yarrow and Sherman (1990) refer to "survivors" as "children [who] have no psychiatric diagnoses, are performing at grade level in school, relate well to peers and adult authorities in school and at home, and have a positive self-concept" (p. 100).

In the present study, resilience is defined as average or above-average performance on a cognitive assessment instrument, falling within a nonclinical range on an emotional/behavioral index completed by the mother, and sound emotional functioning as assessed by a projective drawing test. An emphasis was also placed on observational data pertaining to interactive, motivational, affective, and behavioral functioning.

VULNERABILITY, RISK, AND PROTECTIVE PROCESSES

Anthony (1974) asserts that "whereas risk is a function of the actual physical and psychological environment, vulnerability and invulnerability are states of mind induced in the child by exposure to these risks, and mastery is a force generated in the individual that leads him to test his strength constantly against that of the environment, and to assert himself even against overwhelming odds" (p. 537).

Rutter (1990) asserts that risk factors can be moderated by protective processes. This occurs by reducing the effect of the risk factor on the individual by either altering the meaning the event has for the child or altering the child's exposure to the dangerous situation.

Rutter identifies these interaction effects between risk and moderating or buffering variables as being critical in mediating the relationship between disorder and adaption.

Whereas "risk factors," according to Masten and Garmezy (1985), are related statistically to a higher than expected probability of developing a disorder, "vulnerability" refers to the "susceptibility or predisposition of an individual to negative outcomes" (p. 8). Therefore, vulnerability refers to an individual's predisposition, and risk relates to a group or population factor.

In the area of risk research, Gruenberg (1981) is frequently quoted for the questions he posed, which are: (1) "Who gets sick?"—which encompasses a search for predisposing factors; (2) "Who doesn't get sick?"—which relates to protective factors; and (3) "Why?"—which underscores the importance of identifying risk factors and underlying processes that contribute to favorable or unfavorable outcomes.

Rutter (1979) states, "When the findings are all in, the explanation will probably include the patterning of stresses, individual differences caused by both constitutional and experiential factors, compensating experiences outside the home, the development of self-esteem, the scope and range of available opportunities, an appropriate degree of environmental structure and control, the availability of personal bonds and intimate relationships, and the acquisition of coping skills" (p. 70).

While these broad categories have generally held up over time, further elaboration of the mechanisms involved have been provided by the research of Garmezy (1985), Masten and Garmezy (1985), and Werner and Smith (1982). These researchers have added the following points: (1) the importance of people's appraisal of a situation will to some extent impact on their response; (2) children between the ages of six months and four years have the greatest sensitivity to separation, due to the fact that they have already formed selective attachments but do not yet possess the cognitive capacities to understand the situation; (3) acting reflects a higher level of functioning than reacting; (4) self-efficacy and self-esteem are important correlates of resiliency; (5) secure, stable relationships are important; (6) experiences of mastery, especially those that involve coping successfully with challenging, stressful situations, aid in self-efficacy; and (7) a positive temperamental orientation, especially that of being outgoing and sociable, serves to elicit positive responses from others (Rutter, 1985, p. 608).

SUMMARY OF MAJOR RESEARCH PROJECTS ON RESILIENCY

Kauai Longitudinal Study

The largest and most comprehensive study examining factors associated with resilience was conducted by Werner and colleagues and reported in three volumes (Werner, Bierman, & French, 1971; Werner & Smith, 1977; Werner & Smith 1982). The investigation began in 1954 on a sample of Hawaiian children and has extended over three decades. A sample of 698 children was followed, beginning prenatally and assessed at birth and at ages 1, 2, 10, 18, 30, and 32. The evaluations included observations, interviews, questionnaires, medical examinations, developmental assessments, teachers' reports, and standardized psychological tests.

The study explored the interplay between risk factors within the child and those in the environment. One out of every three infants was considered "at risk" by virtue of perinatal stress, poverty, being reared by mothers with little education, and/or family instability (which included such factors as discord, divorce, parental alcoholism, and mental illness). Three out of four of these early identified children who experienced four or more cumulative risk factors before the age of two subsequently developed serious problems by age ten.

The investigators were most interested in identifying protective factors in the subgroup of high-risk infants who did not develop problems. One out of every four high-risk infants showed resiliency and competency. This group constituted some 10% of the entire sample. Two-year-olds who had been identified as high-risk and who remained resilient (without significant educational or psychosocial problems) at age eighteen were separated into a group, and analyses were performed to determine the factors that aided in their resiliency. The results were published in a volume entitled *Vulnerable But Invincible* (Werner & Smith, 1982).

Initial analyses showed that infants with perinatal complications were no more at risk of later deficits than children with no complications unless they also had other high-risk factors, such as poverty or some other persistent family instability. More than half of the significant predictors were from the first two years of life, while another third were from the period between ages two and ten.

As infants, members of the resilient group had good temperamental characteristics and were often described as "cuddly," "good natured," and "easy to deal with." They were more active than the nonresilient infants, were more able to successfully elicit attention from others, had fewer distressing habits (such as eating and sleeping problems), and recuperated more quickly from illnesses.

As toddlers, the resilient children were described as "alert" and "responsive" and showed significantly greater signs of autonomy. They maintained a positive social orientation with both family and strangers. These children had grown up in smaller families than the nonresilient children and were spaced at least two years apart. They were not likely to have sustained a prolonged separation from their primary caretaker in the first year. The "resilients" had better relationships with their caretakers and had received a good deal of positive support. Their families were described as close and having low levels of conflict. The rules and discipline in their families were clear, and the parents respected the children's autonomy. These families also had a smaller number of chronic stressful life events and a larger social support network.

When caretakers were not available, resilient children were particularly adept at recruiting others and, later in life, selecting resilient models who served as sources of support. These others included peers, older friends, ministers, and teachers.

In elementary school, these children had better reading and reasoning skills and were interested in more activities. Werner (1989) believes that these accomplishments provide the children with a sense of pride and mastery that aids them in their resiliency.

Werner (1989) discovered that, through the first decade of life, boys appear to be substantially more vulnerable than girls. More high-risk girls than boys grow into resilient adolescents. Protective factors are more important for boys. Being first-born is a protective factor for boys, whereas girls prosper if they have a mother who works outside the house and serves as a model. Compared to resilient boys, resilient girls are more assertive and more independent achievers.

Werner and Smith (1982) state that as disadvantage and stressful life experiences increase, "more protective factors in the children and their caregiving environment [are] needed to counterbalance the negative aspects in their lives and ensure a positive developmental outcome" (p. 132). There is always a balance between vulnerabilities, resources, and protective factors within an individual and the social environment in which that individual lives.

Werner (1988) reported that three relatively enduring constellations of protective factors emerged from the analyses made by her and her colleagues. These included: "(1) dispositional attributes of the individual that have a strong genetic base, such as activity level, sociability, and intelligence; (2) affectional ties within the family that provide emotional support in times of stress, either from a parent, grandparent, sibling, mate, or spouse; and (3) informal support systems at school, work, and/or church that reward the individual's competencies, provide a sense of meaning, and foster an internal locus of control" (pp. 4-5).

The Topeka Coping Studies

Murphy and colleagues (Murphy, 1962; Murphy & Moriarty, 1976) followed 32 middle-class Caucasian children from birth through adolescence to study factors related to children's vulnerability and efforts to cope. Their interest was in observing children's responses to naturally occurring stressors such as illnesses, accidents, parental divorce, parental death, and physical trauma. This group also experienced a tornado and the assassination of President Kennedy. While Murphy and colleagues' primary method of evaluation was observational, consistent with a case study approach, they also used standardized assessment instruments.

Murphy and Moriarty (1976) developed a Vulnerability Inventory based on a continuum of functioning and derived from a theoretical basis. Their supposition was that this continuum is relevant to all children and varies according to susceptibility to
internal and external stressors. They divided the inventory into primary (constitutional or early infantile disorders) and secondary (acquired vulnerabilities).

Anthony (1987) describes Murphy and Moriarty's Vulnerability Inventory in the following way:

> The primary vulnerabilities include sensory-motor deficits, deviant body morphology, unusual sensitivities, integrative and adaptive difficulties and imbalances, temperamental deviances, inherent dispositions to passivity, inhibitions, low "sending power," insufficient impulse control, and an incapacity to read caretaker's cues. The secondary vulnerabilities are acquired over the period of development and dispose the child to anxious preoccupations

regarding the functioning of his body, the maintenance of his relationships, the management of ambivalence, and the inability to bear frustration. As a consequence, the child is easily fatigable, unable to relax, and unable to handle energy resources (p. 28).

While overcoming primary vulnerabilities is largely dependent on interaction between child and environment, secondary vulnerabilities frequently result from self-defeating defense mechanisms. Murphy and Moriarty (1976) report that only the most vulnerable infants who experience the severest trauma have long-term developmental problems. Mother's incapacity is noted as a very significant factor in producing drastic changes in the child's adaption.

Murphy and Moriarty (1978) assert that important factors in the process of coping with adversity relate to a child's adequate self-image, sense of security, and positive orientation toward life. They also propose that mother's enjoyment of her child is particularly important because her attitude will manifest in supporting and assisting her child in coping.

Murphy and Moriarty (1976) state, "The parents of good copers neither indulged their children nor overprotected them. They respected their children's capacities, encouraged and rewarded their efforts, and offered reassurance in times of frustration and failure" (p. 349).

The Berkeley Ego Resilience Study

Jeanne and Jack Block (1980) examined the development of ego resilience in a longitudinal study that extended from preschool to late adolescence. They assert that the antecedents of resilience are based in genetic and constitutional factors, as seen in the way infants respond to environmental changes physiologically and temperamentally. Block (1971) also emphasizes the importance of competent, compatible, loving parents in the fostering of resilient children, as opposed to ego-brittle children who are exposed to discord and conflict at home.

The Isle of Wight Study

Rutter and his colleagues (Rutter, 1979; Rutter, Cox, Tupling, Berger, & Yule, 1975; Rutter, Yule, Quinton, Rowlands, Yule, & Berger, 1975) conducted an epidemiological study on the Isle of Wight and in an inner London borough. They compared the incidence of psychiatric disorder in ten-year-old children residing in these two very different locations.

In the course of their research, they identified six "risk" factors associated with a heightened prevalence of psychiatric disorder in children. These include: (1) severe marital discord; (2) low social status of the family; (3) overcrowding or large family size; (4) parental criminality; (5) maternal psychiatric disorder; and (6) admission of the child into the care of a local authority (i.e., placement outside the family).

Protective factors that ameliorate a child's risk status include: positive temperament; girls are more resilient than boys; parental warmth, affection and absence of criticism from at least one parent (even if there is significant parental discord); and a supportive, encouraging school environment that aids in development of the child's values and competence. Rutter identifies a child's self-concept as being an important correlate of resiliency. Not only are children with high self-esteem better able to negotiate stressful experiences, but they also elicit more positive feedback from their environment, which in turn promotes mastery.

Rutter (1979) categorized families in his study according to the number of risk factors present. He reports that when a child is exposed to a single stressor, even if chronic, the child is no more at risk than those children who are exposed to no risk factors at all. However, when a child is exposed to two or three risk factors simultaneously, the level of psychiatric risk increases fourfold. With four risk factors and above, the level of psychiatric risk increases tenfold.

The stresses of additive risk factors raise adverse rates multiplicatively, not additively. In other words, stresses potentiate each other so their effect is much greater than the summation effects considered singly. This finding suggests that the specific type of stressor may not be as critical as the shear number of stressors.

The Minnesota High-Risk Studies

A number of studies have been conducted in Minnesota by Garmezy and his colleagues (Garmezy, 1983, 1985; Garmezy, Masten, & Tellegen, 1984; Garmezy & Tellegen, 1984) over the past twenty years, searching for protective factors in high-risk, "stress resistant" children.

In the beginning, Nuechterlein (1970), under the supervision of Garmezy, completed a literature survey of studies of competent

African-American children from low socioeconomic homes. A summary of the findings was described by Garmezy (1981). Some of these findings include: (1) competent children are well-liked by their peers and adults and are rated by teachers as possessing social skills; (2) they tend to have a positive sense of self and a sense of personal power, as opposed to powerlessness; (3) an internal locus of control suggests that these children feel a sense of control over their environment; (4) the children show reflectiveness and impulse control; (5) in single-parent families, it is the mother's ability to compensate for an absent father, rather than father absence alone, that is most predictive; (6) a degree of order, in addition to the presence of stimulating resources in the home, is important; (7) parents who assist with homework and see the value of education have more competent children; (8) role definitions between parents and children are made clear (children are not expected to meet parents' needs, and parents are appropriate authority figures) (9) parents provide children with self-direction and are aware of their children's interests and goals; and (10) children have at least one adequate identification figure in their lives (pp. 220-221).

Garmezy (1983) identifies three consistent categories of variables that enhance stress resistance in children. These categories, which are similar to those of Rutter et al. (1975) and Werner and Smith (1982), include: (1) dispositional attributes of the child (e.g., temperament, positive social orientation, self-esteem, and hardiness); (2) family cohesion and absence of family discord and neglect; and (3) the availability and utilization of external support systems that reinforce a child's coping efforts.

NIMH Child-Rearing Study

Radke-Yarrow and Sherman (1990) examined genetic and environmental risk conditions in 123 primarily middle-class, Caucasian families in which the mother or both parents were depressed or in which both parents were without a psychiatric disorder. They identified several key factors in "child survivors." The factors they specify include: (1) there is a match between a psychological or physical quality in a child and a core need that the child fulfills in one or both of the parents; and (2) the child has a sense that there is something good and special about himself or herself that is not only a source of positive self-regard for the child but also serves a need-satisfying role for the parent (p. 112). "Child survivors" were all described by their parents as "attractive," "charming," "socially engaging," "alert," and "curious," in addition to having been identified as possessing above-average intelligence.

Long-Term Patient and Family Studies

Bleuler (1978) studied the long-term adjustment of a sample of children of parents who were diagnosed as schizophrenic. He found that even though many of the children had endured very difficult childhoods, only a minority of them were deemed incompetent. His impression, as cited in Rutter (1987), is that "protection may lie in the 'steeling' qualities that derive from successful coping with the hazards when the exposure is of a type and degree that is manageable in the context of the child's capacities and social situation" (p. 326).

The Rochester Longitudinal Study

The purpose of this study, which began in 1970, was to investigate the early development of children who were at risk due to maternal psychopathology. It was a prospective longitudinal investigation that began during the mother's pregnancy and continued through early childhood (Sameroff, Barocas, & Seifer, 1984). The subjects included 337 women who carried the diagnoses of schizophrenia or depression or who manifested a personality disorder. The control group contained women who were matched on the variables of age, race, socioeconomic status, number of children, education, and sex of child. The control group subjects were thought to have no history of mental illness.

Sameroff and Seifer (1983) concluded that, among the mental illness groups, severity and chronicity of disturbance is more predictive than specific diagnosis. They also noted that social status has a major moderating effect.

Utilizing data from the Rochester Longitudinal Study, Sameroff, Seifer, Barocas, Zax, and Greenspan (1987) identified ten individual risk factors, which they developed into a multiple risk index. The index includes: maternal mental health functioning (chronicity); anxiety; perspectives on child-rearing; education; occupation; minority status; interaction style; family support; life events; and family size. These factors were chosen to encompass the categories of: (1) psychological functioning of the mother; (2) the status of the family; and (3) the broader cultural context in which the family lives. Of interest is the fact that no child-centered factors were included in the multiple risk analyses.

The researchers reported that with a sample of 215 four-year-old children who had been followed since conception, a composite risk score predicts verbal IQ much better than any single factor alone. As the number of risk factors increases, performance decreases, with extreme categories differing by over 30 IQ points.

Socioeconomic status was highlighted as a potential psychosocial risk factor, even though it was noted that risk factors tend to cluster in poor families. In the highest socioeconomic status (SES) group, with zero to one risk factors, the mean verbal IQ score was 120, compared to a mean verbal IQ score of 113 in the low SES group. These findings are similar to those of Werner and Smith (1982), who reported that children from high SES homes with the most severe perinatal problems have mean IQ's similar to those of poor children with no perinatal complications.

Similarly, in a study conducted on children from the Collaborative Project, which examined the effects of stress on IQ in a sample of 4,154 seven-year-old children, Brown and Rosenbaum (1984) reported an inverted-U curve for performance on the Wechsler Intelligence Scale for Children (WISC) versus stress measured by total number of problems per child. The same U-curve is seen for the low SES children as for the high SES children, but it peaks at lower stress levels, suggesting higher arousal and more stress.

In a follow-up study of 26,760 biracial infants enrolled in the National Collaborative Perinatal Project, Broman, Nichols, and Kennedy (1975) reported that SES and maternal education are better predictors of children's intellectual performance as measured by the Stanford-Binet Form L-M at age four than type or degree of neonatal illness.

CHARACTERISTICS OF THE CHILD

Several researchers have emphasized attributes of the child as having a major impact on whether a child is resilient or not under adverse conditions (Garmezy, 1987; Rutter, 1985; Werner & Smith, 1982). When studies have taken into account child attributes, in addition to environmental factors and life stress, a considerably greater proportion of variance in adjustment has been accounted for. Multiple correlation coefficients between .60 and .80 have been reported (Garmezy, Masten,

& Tellegen, 1984; Seifer & Sameroff, 1987; Wertlieb, Weigel, Springer, & Feldstein, 1989).

Temperament

Children of differing temperaments elicit different parental behaviors. When parents are living under extremely stressful conditions, they can easily become overwhelmed by a temperamentally difficult child. Crockenberg (1981) asserts that social support has the greatest impact for mothers with temperamentally difficult children and the lowest impact for mothers with babies who are emotionally calm. She reports that easy babies are more securely attached even when "potentially unfavorable social milieus exist" (p. 862).

Temperamentally easy babies are described as having positive mood, regular physiological functioning, low reactivity, and rapid adaption to new situations (Thomas, Chess, Birch, Hertzig, & Korn, 1963). The ease with which these babies can be cared for increases a mother's self-esteem and sense of competency and leads to a more satisfying relationship. Temperamentally easy children both avoid negative interactions (Rutter, 1978, 1979) and are better able to cope with conflict when it is present (Rutter, 1979).

Goldberg (1977), cited in Werner & Smith (1982), asserts that parental perceptions of the infant's demeanor are the best predictors of the interaction between parent and child. Resilient babies in Werner & Smith's (1982) study are identified by attributes that are rewarding to caretakers. Not only do these babies freely initiate contact and respond socially, but they are also described by parents and professionals as "very active," "good natured," "easy to deal with," and "cuddly and affectionate." Murphy and Moriarty (1976) describe active babies as better copers because they have the potential for capturing the attention of an unresponsive parent.

Difficult children are described as having low thresholds for arousal, intense reactions when aroused, and irregular biological functioning (Thomas, Chess, & Birch, 1968). Rutter (1990) adds low malleability, negative mood, and low fastidiousness to the description of children with adverse temperaments. Hetherington (1984) states that "temperamentally difficult children have been found to be less adaptive to change and more vulnerable to adversity than are temperamentally easy children" (pp. 22-23). Vulnerable infants are also described as unusually inactive, possessing less ability to engage others, crying more and for longer periods, are less easily soothed, and require more caretaking (Anthony, 1987; Provence, 1974). These infants have the potential for easily overwhelming their mothers, resulting in negative repercussions for the relationship.

Research by Rutter (1979) and Rutter, Quinton, and Yule (1977) reveal that temperamentally difficult children, as opposed to temperamentally easy children, are more likely to be the target of parental hostility and criticism. When parents become depressed or irritable, they are more likely to take their anger out selectively on the difficult child. Difficult temperament is also identified in several studies as a factor in eliciting maltreatment (Belsky, 1980; Sameroff & Chandler, 1975; Vietze, Falsey, Sandler, O'Connor, & Altemier, 1980).

Constitution

Children exhibit varying thresholds for stimuli. While some children appear vulnerable from early in infancy, others present as robust, energetic, interested, and trustful. It has been suggested that a vulnerability to becoming overwhelmed traumatically may have a constitutional basis (Fenichel, 1945).

Anthony (1987) explains that each child differs in his or her response to environmental stress. Some children appear hypervulnerable, having difficulty recovering from stressful situations, while other children rebound rapidly and appear generally unaffected.

Freud (1922), as cited in Anthony (1987), put forth a concept of a protective shield against stimuli that serves a buffering function between the self and the outer world. Lacking such a protective shield, Virginia Woolf (1971) as cited in Anthony and Cohler (1987) described herself as "skinless," suffering from an "appalling sense of vulnerability" (p. 25).

Drawing on Freud's theory, Anthony (1987) states, in relation to his work with resilient children, that the child "acquires a skin that functions as a resistant membrane or special envelope. Because of this shield, the strong stimuli from the outer world are able to penetrate the living organism, but with only a small fraction of their actual intensity" (p. 11).

Birth Status

Myers and King (1983) hypothesized that "black children from poverty backgrounds begin to develop, even *in utero*, in chronically stressed environments" (p. 293). These authors believe that African-Americans are likely to function at a higher basal stress level, even in utero, as a result of a myriad of social stressors including racism. They postulate that this may account for their greater vulnerability to stress.

Poor pregnant women are more likely than other women to receive late or no prenatal care and to deliver a low birthweight baby or one who is more likely to be disabled or die in infancy (Children's Defense Fund, 1991). African-American children are at the highest risk, with infant mortality rates exceeding those of all other groups (Children's Defense Fund, 1991). Oakland has one of the highest rates of infant death in the nation. In the city's poorer districts, the rate is 17.97 per 1,000 births versus 10.00 per 1,000 nationwide. The African-American infant mortality rate in this country is 17.6 per 1,000 versus the white infant mortality rate of 8.5 per 1,000 (National Center for Health Statistics, 1988).

All indicators point to the fact that homeless women are at the highest risk for receiving late, minimal, or no prenatal care and subsequently delivering a high-risk baby. If a woman does not know where she is going to sleep or how she is going to feed and buy basic necessities for her other children, prenatal care is not going to be her top priority. If a homeless woman is abusing substances, as a high percentage are (Emergency Services Network of Alameda County, 1990), she will avoid prenatal care because of her primary commitment to drugs, her guilt, and her fear that the infant will be taken from her at birth. In addition, the very conditions that increase perinatal risk (malnutrition, consumption of drugs and alcohol, and illness) are over-represented among homeless populations (Kopp, 1983).

Pasamanick and Knobloch (1960) describe a continuum of reproductive insult, which in part is determined by socioeconomic status. Shonkoff (1982), as cited in Parker, Greer, and Zuckerman (1988), states that children living in poverty "carry a disproportionate burden of biologic vulnerability that is largely related to the increased health risks of poverty" (p. 1231).

Some researchers assert that risk factors can be overcome with the right caregiving environment. Werner, Bierman, and French (1971) refer to at-risk children as "environmental casualties" rather than "perinatal casualties." Numerous studies have pointed to SES as a modifier of prenatal risk: there is a protective influence for high SES children, while low SES children are at increased risk (Kopp & Krakow, 1983; Sameroff & Chandler, 1975; Werner & Smith, 1982).

O'Dougherty and Wright (1989), commenting on the results of Werner and colleagues' longitudinal study, state, "Severe perinatal stress was associated with later impairments of cognitive, physical, or emotional functioning only when accompanied by adverse environmental circumstances" (p. 122).

Kopp and Kaler (1989) wrote about biological risks which could adversely affect development beginning in infancy. They stated, "When genetic heritage and prenatal life are favorable, the infant's roots are securely anchored and sound development should occur" (p.224). In sum, birth status and the subsequent caregiving environment have significant effects on a child's temperament and constitution, which in turn significantly affect a child's potential to thrive.

Prenatal Exposure to Crack-Cocaine

There is general agreement among researchers that it is too early to determine the long-term effects of prenatal drug exposure, particularly cocaine, on children. At this point in time, there are not enough well-controlled longitudinal studies. While exposure to substances *in utero* may produce a continuum of adverse conditions, there is no consensus in the literature as to whether these conditions will persist beyond infancy or if they will be present at all.

Review articles by Myers, Britt, Lodder, Kendall, and Williams-Peterson (1992) and Neuspiel and Hamel (1991), report two consistent findings in the research they reviewed on *in utero* drug-exposed children. These include: (1) children are more at risk for being born prematurely; and (2) children are of lower birthweight, birth length, head circumference, and size for gestational age. These studies note that while prenatally drug-exposed children are at risk for these anomalies, the vast majority of infants show no such impairments.

Certain consistent difficulties in drug-exposed infants and toddlers have been reported. These include: tremulousness and irritability (Chasnoff, Burns, Schnoll, & Burns, 1985; Dow-Edwards, 1988; Finnegan, Mellott, Ryan, & Wapner, 1989; Oro & Dixon, 1987); poor affect regulation (Howard, 1989); a tendency to become overwhelmed by environmental stimuli (Chasnoff et al., 1985); limitations in interactive behavior (Howard, 1989; Van Dyke & Fox 1990); and poor state regulation (Chasnoff et al., 1985; Weston, Ivins, Zuckerman, Jones, & Lopez, 1989).

Dixon and Bejar (1989) assert that evidence of brain damage in drug-exposed children may appear only when more complex processing tasks involving visual-motor skills are required, around the time that children enter school.

The trouble with making a causal association between *in utero* drug exposure and children's subsequent neurodevelopmental deficits is that there are so many confounding environmental factors. Drug-dependent mothers are frequently depressed and anxious and typically live in very stressful environments. Factors such as limited financial resources, inadequate or no housing, poor nutrition, late, no, or irregular prenatal care, and use of additional substances such as tobacco, alcohol, marijuana, and other drugs, are likely to have synergistic effects on child outcomes. Many users of crack-cocaine have reported that their craving for the drug often supersedes all other activities, including tending to a child once born.

Gender

Research consistently shows that boys are more at risk than girls under stressful conditions. Boys are more physically vulnerable at birth (Rutter, 1981, 1984; Rutter, Maughan, Mortimore, Ouston, & Smith, 1979; Werner & Smith, 1982); are more likely to develop behavioral disorders when exposed to family discord (Porter & O'Leary, 1980; Rutter, 1970, 1981, 1982; Werner & Smith, 1982); are more vulnerable following the birth of a sibling (Dunn, Kendrick, & MacNamee, 1981; Hetherington, 1984); and are more adversely affected by day care (Hetherington, 1984; Rutter, 1981), by mother working outside the home (Werner & Smith, 1982), and by father absence (Rutter, 1970; Werner & Smith, 1982).

Murphy and Moriarty (1976) report that resilient boys, compared to resilient girls, have fewer stressful life events and live in families with fewer children and less crowding. In all cases, the father has been present in the home. In addition, being firstborn matters more for boys than girls.

Several explanations have been put forth in an attempt to explain these findings. Schulz (1977) asserts that mothers' exploitative relationships with men may influence their feelings toward their sons. Elder (1979) reports that mothers are far less protective of their sons than their daughters. This is particularly true for impoverished families. Hetherington (1980) observed that parents are more likely to quarrel in front of their sons than their daughters when there is severe conflict. Rutter (1990) suggests that protection in being a girl may have more to do with a reduced exposure to conflictual family interactions.

Resilient children appear to do best when they have role models who complement their gender (Murphy & Moriarty, 1976). Girls benefit most from, and are drawn to, autonomous and independent role models. They prosper when they have a mother who works outside the home who can serve as a competent and effective role model. Boys, on the other hand, benefit most from receiving a great deal of nurturance and care (Werner & Smith, 1982).

Same-sex identification is also important for both girls and boys. Werner and Smith (1982) report that maternal mental health is more important for girls, whereas boys need an available father figure. Boys, they assert, are more at risk living in a single-parent, female-headed household where the mother works outside the home (Werner & Smith, 1982).

Pianta, Egeland, and Sroufe (1990) similarly report that girls are more affected by the coping styles of their mothers, whereas boys are more affected by the quality of the home environment and the mother-child interaction. Resilient mothers' positive mental health (absence of anxiety or depression), these authors assert, is very important to the development of competence in girls.

THE MOTHER-CHILD RELATIONSHIP

Availability, Attunement, Attachment

The importance of the mother-infant relationship for a child's subsequent personality development has been documented throughout the literature. A foundation of security is set down early in childhood, which has far-reaching implications for self-concept, self-esteem, autonomy, and the extent to which later relationships can be formed (Bowlby, 1973; Sroufe & Fleeson, 1986). This early relationship has been shown to serve as a degree of protection against future stressful situations (Rutter, 1987). Research has shown that infants with secure attachments are better able to cope, are more intelligent, and more socially competent (Easterbrooks & Lamb, 1979; Hazen & Durrett, 1982; Matas, Arend, & Sroufe, 1978; Thompson & Lamb, 1983).

Rutter (1985) asserts, "What seems important for protection [of a child] is a secure relationship with someone" (p. 603). Factors that have been shown to be important in developing such a relationship include warmth, sensitivity, accessibility, and interest. Winnicott (1960) emphasizes the need for consistency and continuity in his description of "good enough mothering." Another important aspect of "good enough" care involves having a caretaker who is attuned enough to her infant to be sensitive to reading the infant's signals and responding in a way that soothes the infant (Ainsworth, Bell, & Stayton, 1971; Schaffer & Emerson, 1964; Stayton & Ainsworth, 1973). As these interactions build up over time, the relationship becomes more secure. Spitz (1957) refers to this process as "the dialogue," which aids in developing confidence (Benedek, 1956) and optimism (Erikson, 1950).

A "sensitive period" begins at about six months, when development of strong affectional bonds take place. Rutter (1978) suggests that selective bonding must take place during the first two years because children are much less likely to develop for the first time a selective, secure bond after age three or four. While a secure bond can be transferred if lost, it is not likely to be initially formed after this time.

Sensitive responsiveness is the quality that is most likely to foster a secure attachment (Bowlby, 1969). An attachment figure is viewed as providing a "secure base," a sense of protection for the child. A secure bond helps children deal with frightening situations because they have built up confidence in a caregiver over time. Stayton and Ainsworth (1973) define a secure attachment as enabling children to feel safe in strange situations.

While dependency needs can be taken care of by many different people, attachment has been defined by some researchers as confined to one or two people (Gewirtz, 1972, 1976). This is a point of debate in the attachment literature. Kalish and Knudtson (1976) advocate extending the idea of attachment to include other important people, places, and things beyond the primary caretakers. Ainsworth (1972) similarly argues that attachments should include siblings and close friends. In many impoverished families, this seems particularly relevant when younger children are commonly raised by older siblings.

Each child, state George and Solomon (1989), citing Bowlby's (1979) and Bretherton's (1985) work, develops "internal working models" of the environment and of the self in relation to the environment. These models are based on actual experiences that the child has had with attachment figures. The models include expectations of others' responsiveness (e.g., "My mother will comfort me when I need her") and an image of how acceptable they are in the eyes of their attachment figure (e.g., "I am worthy of care") (George & Solomon, 1989, p. 225). Models of self and world are complementary. A mother's availability and responsiveness equate with a child's own sense of acceptability, self-esteem, and confidence in the environment. The child learns that the world is either responsive or unresponsive, threatening or benign.

When mothers are able to read their infants' cues and respond appropriately to their infants' developmental needs, the infants gradually, via mirroring (Kohut, 1977), become aware of themselves and their own feelings. What is important is that the infants have learned that they can have an impact on their environment. Mothers' responses reinforce their infants' active coping strategies (Yarrow, Rubenstein, & Pedersen, 1975). This enables children who feel vulnerable to feel capable of triggering a protective process (Garmezy & Masten, 1991).

What Spitz (1957) calls a "derailment of dialogue" refers to a situation in which a child sends signals but receives no response. The caretaker's unresponsiveness could be due to fatigue, depression, substance abuse, or other simultaneous life stressors (Coppolillo, 1987). When signalling fails, an infant typically withdraws and, over time, gives up attempting to elicit a response. This dynamic can be seen as an early form of learned helplessness (Seligman, 1975).

Insecure attachments result from actual separations or fear of separation. Life stress has been shown to interfere with the mother-infant attachment process (Vaughan, Egeland, Sroufe, & Waters, 1979). Infants with insecure attachments have not developed a sense of security, are more prone to anxiety, feel less protected, are more vulnerable, and have a tendency to remain detached from emotional experiences (Bowlby, 1969). Insecure attachments have been associated in many studies with the development of later psychopathology (Arend, Gove, & Sroufe, 1979; Lewis, Feiring, McGuffog, & Jaskir, 1984), and loss of attachment figures in childhood has been theorized to be an important antecedent of depression (Bowlby, 1973).

Murphy (1987) describes the importance of a child's early experiences impacting later development in the following way. He states:

> The roots of optimism lie in infancy—in the repeated experiences of gratification of needs, of being able to count on life feeling good. The optimism and hope that come from the earliest satisfying, restorative

experiences are reinforced in the next few years when separations are followed by reunions, frustrations bring support in coping, pain is followed by comfort, initiatives are backed up, and the child develops confidence that he and the environment will be able to manage any problem (p. 104).

Caretakers' ability to buffer their children from experiences that they are not yet developmentally able to cope with assists the children to develop confidence. This is a nearly impossible task for a homeless family. Young children are exposed to many situations and circumstances that they have little ability to defend themselves against. Children in such stressful conditions require more actual physical presence of the caregiver and what Bower (1977) refers to as the "mediating parent." Masten and Garmezy (1985) cite a number of studies that refer to an "environmental protective barrier embodied in the mother" (p. 9), which can serve as a protective shield for the child against stress. Homeless mothers, however, have little protection themselves and can, at times, feel as vulnerable, needy, and dependent as their children (Boxill & Beaty, 1990).

Beyond a secure relationship, children need feedback on how their behavior is affecting their environment so they can learn to discern contingencies, regulate their behavior, and internalize norms. The ability to develop self-control is dependent on the environment not being too impinging, overstimulating, or disorganized.

RISK FACTORS

Issues Related to the Homeless Experience

Few children or parents are left untouched by an experience of homelessness. Goodman, Saxe, and Harvey (1991) assert that loss of housing can produce psychological trauma. It is the end result of having used up or depleted network resources. Brown and Ziefert (1990) state, "For women the loss of housing can signify an end to the safety and familiarity symbolized by a home that provides [the family] with the rootedness from which they master the tasks of daily living" (p. 11). Baumann and Grigsby (1988) state that homelessness is not merely the loss of housing but that "homeless persons face the potential loss of almost everything they have—most importantly a sense of belonging, a psychological sense of home" (p. 15).

The limited options available to homeless individuals serve to erode their sense of self-efficacy and put into question their ability to care for themselves and their children. Wherever they go, they often feel unwanted and have lost a sense of safety, security, and privacy. They also are likely to have lost any social bonds that they may have had.

While there are few studies on the effects of homelessness, it is generally assumed that the homeless experience has far-reaching effects on mothers, children, and the relationship between the two of them. Hausman and Hammen (1993) assert that the experience of homelessness presents homeless families with a double crisis: the trauma of losing a home in addition to "impediments to a parent's ability to function as a consistent and supportive caregiver" (p. 358).

Koplow (1996) writes about the impersonal environment homeless parents and children are thrust into. She states, "The homeless parent cannot provide an intimate environment from which to nurture and structure her child. She cannot act on her attunement to her own needs or to the child's needs" (p.220). She goes on to say that homeless families "struggle to remain connected to one another in spite of the lack of shelter for their relationship" (p. 219).

Molnar (1991) sums the situation up this way: "The evidence is clear: rootlessness, chaos, no place—literally—to call home; these conditions are inimical to healthy child development" (p. 4).

Homeless children are exposed to behaviors and environments from which their parents cannot protect them. Some of these include unsanitary conditions, promiscuity, drug abuse, violence, and individuals with severe mental health problems. Such conditions create severe emotional trauma, especially for young children, who are faced with challenges that are beyond their coping abilities. Young children are still very dependent on parents and need a more structured and predictable environment than older children.

Young children are less able to understand negative events and possible outcomes, whereas older children have the cognitive capacities to interpret the environment better.

Anthony (1987) refers to "representational competence" as a child's capacity to make "meaningful sense" out of the chaotic events in the environment: "Representational competence is concerned with how far the child acquires understanding of what is going on around him, the assumption being that such acquisitions help the child to master the stress" (p. 22). Children are not only more able to understand their environment with increasing age, but also develop a range of coping behaviors and resources so that they

are not so dependent on others for protection. With increasing age, children can remove themselves from distressing situations, reducing their risk to exposure.

Young children's personalities are in the process of being formed. It has been postulated that early life experiences alter subsequent development and responses to stress. For example, Pianta, Egeland, and Sroufe (1990) assert that concurrent stress is not as significant in determining a child's developmental outcome as stress experienced early in the child's development. Spending their formative years in dangerous and stressful environments, such as living in shelters, on the streets, or doubled up with other families, is sure to be trauma-producing for the vast majority of children.

Boxill (1989) states, "The daily emotional struggles and dilemmas of being homeless are intense and difficult and inappropriate for young children" (p. 57). The Coro Foundation (1991) reports that almost 70% of the parents they surveyed in eleven shelters in Alameda County, California, stated that living in a shelter had "affected their relationship with their kids in a negative way" (p. 14). One parent in the study stated, "It's really tough trying to be a good parent in this place. I don't have enough quality one-on-one time with my kids because I'm constantly stressed and sad and worried" (p. 15).

Boxill (1989) notes that children's "confidence in their parents' ability to negotiate the larger society is shaken," and states that they "often internalize a sense of being adrift" (p. 61). Williams (1991) reports that social workers in Los Angeles County noted children's immense rage directed at their parents because of their perceived lack of power and their own heightened sense of vulnerability. They state, "The parents were viewed by their children as unable to help themselves, unable to help their children, and unable to manage their world" (p. 295). The condition of homelessness, according to Koplow (1996), "deprives the child of experiencing his or her parent as provider or protector" (p. 220).

Children are impacted most by a loss of home due to their developmental need for nurturance and consistency. Their basic need for safety, security, self-esteem, a sense of belonging, and attachment may be significantly disrupted. Even basic daily routines such as sleeping and eating are significantly altered.

Boxill and Beaty (1990) have identified six themes from their observations of homeless families.

Theme 1: "Intense Desire to Demonstrate Internalized Values as a Way of Asserting Self." Children have been observed to be notably protective of their self-esteem. They assert their needs and values as a way of holding on to their self-worth in the identity-threatening environment of the shelter.

Theme 2: "Questioning the Certainty of Anything, the Ambiguity of Everything." Nothing in homeless children's lives is stable. They frequently move from shelter to shelter among strangers. Routines that they may have counted on when they were housed are no longer predictable. Pavenstedt (1967) states, "They do not have inner confidence that they will not suddenly be whacked or humiliated or deserted, or that the situation will not unexpectedly change" (p. 131).

Theme 3: "Conflict over the Need for Attention and the Experienced Demand for Independence." This theme is similar to the rapprochement stage that Mahler, Pine, and Bergman (1975) describe, in which children are observed to dart back and forth between mothers' and surrogate-mothers' laps and independent play. This behavior has been interpreted as a message from children to mothers that they still need them but are also capable of being independent and taking care of themselves.

Theme 4: "Mothers' Themes—Public Mothering." Since living in shelters affords little privacy, women are forced, in the words of Boxill and Beaty (1990), to "do their mothering in the company and in full view of others" (p. 52), which has grave consequences for the mother-child relationship. These authors note that "every aspect and nuance of the mother-child relationship occurs and is affected by its public and often scrutinized nature" (p. 58).

Theme 5: "Unraveling of the Mother Role." Mothers living in shelters have little authority over establishing rules for their children. Shelter staff typically designate mealtimes and bedtimes and frequently even intervene in discipline. Some children form indiscriminate attachments as a result of being mothered by so many different people.

Mihaly (1991) states, "Research has shown that this usurpation of parental roles is depressing and confusing both to parents and children and may have effects that last far beyond the episode of homelessness itself" (p. 27). It is unclear, at this time, what long-term effects depriving mothers of the opportunity to perform their parental role has on their children's ability to regain trust in them and reestablish, or form for the first time, a secure bond. Role reversal is commonly observed whereby children are seen comforting their mothers. Boxill and Beaty (1990) assert that due to having little protection themselves, homeless mothers can, at times, feel as vulnerable, needy, and

dependent as their children. They state, "Mothers appeared to have temporarily become children along with their children" (p. 60).

Theme 6: "The Experience of Being Externally Controlled." The shared feeling among homeless mothers is that they have lost all control over manipulating their environment. Routines and decisions are determined primarily by others. This externalized structure places homeless women in the position of feeling very helpless.

Other aspects of the homeless experience that are detrimental to children's development include: the lack of personal space (Proshansky & Gottlieb, 1989); the loss of one's own possessions, which serve to anchor and give a sense of belonging and rootedness (Rivlin, 1990); the problem of crowding, which is detrimental because there is no place to which children can retreat (Saegert, 1981; Wolfe, 1978); a high level of noise, which interferes with children's ability to distinguish between speech sounds and to learn to read, due to a tendency to tune out auditory cues (Cohen, Glass, & Singer, 1973); and the oftentimes dangerous conditions that restrict children's play, having negative repercussions for children's health and physical, emotional, and cognitive development (Berezin, 1988).

Children living in these crowded, overstimulating conditions have been witnessed to either withdraw emotionally or become aggressive (Parke, 1978; Wolfe, 1978). They cannot learn to discern contingencies, regulate their behavior and internalize norms because the environment is too impinging, anxiety-provoking, and disorganized. Furthermore, parents living in crowded accommodations have been reported to use more punitive child-rearing practices (Newson & Newson, 1963; Roy, 1950).

Children from homeless families are at greater risk of being placed outside their mother's care than children who live in poverty. One report (National Black Child Development Institute, 1989) found that

38% of children placed in foster care in six cities had been placed as a result of housing-related problems, including homelessness.

The Impact of Poverty on Parenting

Among poor families, life is a daily struggle with inadequate resources. Chronic poverty is not a unitary event but a conglomerate of stressful life conditions that are pervasive and not bounded (Makosky, 1982; Ray & McLoyd, 1986). Multiple simultaneous stressors are more devastating than single, separate, stressful life events (Neiman, 1988).

In poor families, there is an over-representation of frustration-producing events (Liem & Liem, 1978); more long-term chronic life conditions (Belle, 1984; Brown, Bhrolchain, & Harris, 1975; Liem & Liem, 1978); and an unremitting succession of negative life events that leave little time for recuperation (Belle, 1984) and often precipitate additional life crises (Makosky, 1982).

Poor families live under very oppressive conditions with very few protective barriers. They are subjected to daily hassles, which include having to deal with all sorts of institutions, such as the welfare system, the Housing Authority, and Child Protective Services. Interacting with these systems can be very demeaning and dehumanizing (Goodban, 1985; Marshall, 1982; Pearlin & Johnson, 1977) and contribute to poor psychological status (Belle, 1982; Goodman, Saxe, & Harvey, 1991; McLoyd, 1990; McLoyd & Wilson, 1990).

Families living in poverty have very few choices. They are not free to decide what neighborhood they are going to live in, what schools they are going to send their children to, and where they will be able to get health care. They are also more subject to being controlled by others (McLoyd, 1990). All of these dynamics culminate in families feeling emotionally downtrodden. Galambos and Silbereisen (1987) assert that pessimism about life increases as income decreases. McLoyd and Wilson (1990) report that there is a strong link between economic hardship and diminished psychological well-being.

Caretakers who are experiencing increased stress become less supportive, involved, and nurturant due to their own overwhelming needs. Anthony (1987) states, "A mother under stress can become a multimodel of stimulus distress, which shows itself in her facial expressions, the tone of voice, the touching, the carrying, and the caring" (p. 30)."

Bandler (1967) observed that, under highly stressful conditions, "the needs of the parents take precedence over the needs of the children. For this reason, among many others, the mothers cannot be adequate models for their children or provide the experiences necessary for growth and development" (p. 231). Not only do parents tend to be less supportive, involved, and nurturant living under oppressed conditions, but they are more likely to use power-assertive techniques such as physical punishment and less likely to use reasoning and negotiation (McLoyd, 1990; Patterson, 1988; Patterson, DeBaryshe, & Ramsey, 1989; Wilson, 1974).

Several studies reveal that parents resort to violence when they feel they have lost control of their own lives (Spinetta & Rigler, 1972), when they experience economic loss (Steinberg, Catalano, & Dooley, 1981), or when they become homeless (Alperstein, Rappaport, & Flanigan, 1988; Meiselman, 1978). Unemployment has been found to have grave consequences for families. It has been associated with father-child sexual abuse (Meiselman, 1978), spousal battering (Straus, Gelles, & Steinmetz, 1980), depression, anxiety, hostility, increased alcohol consumption, and increased pessimism about life (Galambos & Silbereisen, 1987; McLoyd, 1990), and the use of less nurturant and more punitive and arbitrary interactions with children (McLoyd, 1989).

Finkelhor (1983) describes a common phenomenon whereby abuse is acted out in an attempt to compensate for a perceived lack or loss of power. In expressing violence, there is an attempt to regain power. The anger resulting from a man's perceived helpless position is displaced onto his wife and children. Research shows that the greatest amount of abuse is directed toward the most powerless individuals, particularly children under the age of six (Gil, 1979; Maden & Wrench, 1977; Straus, Gelles, & Steinmetz, 1980). As Finkelhor et al. (1983) state, "Abuse tends to gravitate toward the relationships of greatest power differential" (p. 18). Abusers can have powerful effects on shaping victims' perceptions. When the abuser is an influential person in a child's life, the child commonly sees himself or herself as having provoked the abuse or having deserved it, no matter how arbitrary it is (Finkelhor, 1983).

Research shows that expressions of anger cause severe distress in young children, threatening their sense of security (Jaffe, Wolfe, & Wilson, 1990). Children from violent homes are reported to have impaired social competence (Wolfe, Zak, Wilson, & Jaffe, 1986) and behavior problems (Hughes & Barad, 1982; Rosenbaum & O'Leary, 1981).

Perhaps the greatest consequence to children who are victims of violence, or who witness it, is that they learn that violence is an acceptable way of resolving conflict (Jaffe, Wolfe, & Wilson, 1990). They also do not learn appropriate controls for aggression (Wolfe, Zak, Wilson, & Jaffe, 1986) and are at risk of "identifying with the aggressor," which involves modeling their behavior after their abusers (Garbarino et al., 1991).

Risk Status Associated with Single Motherhood

Single parenthood represents a significant stressor. Mothers are not only vulnerable to social isolation, but have sole responsibility for raising children without the emotional or financial support of a father. These families are often forced to rely on Aid for Families with Dependent Children (AFDC) benefits, which are very inadequate.

Single mothers are at greater risk than other mothers for anxiety, depression, and developing health problems. The effects are intensified when single mothers live alone and are destitute (Garfinkel & McLanahan, 1986; Guttentag, Salasin, & Belle, 1980; Taylor, Chatters, Tucker, & Lewis, 1991). Pearlin and Johnson (1977) state, "The combination most productive of psychological distress is to be simultaneously single, isolated, exposed to burdensome parental obligations—and most serious of all—poor" (p. 714).

Tucker (1978), as cited in McLoyd (1990), similarly reports that, "Being single, poor, young, and black was the combination most productive of dissatisfied parenting and lack of parental fulfillment" (p. 320). Thompson and Ensminger (1989) assert that for poor black women, long-term single parenting represents a chronic stressor. This is particularly true for homeless families that are primarily headed by a young single parent (Wood, Valdez, Hayashi, & Shen, 1990).

According to Hetherington (1984), the following dynamics place women and children at high risk: "the lack of availability of the noncustodial parent; and the presence of fewer significant adults in the household to participate in decision making, to serve
as models, disciplinarians, as sources of nurturance, or to assume responsibility for childcare and household tasks" (p. 21).

Kellam, Ensminger, and Turner (1977) examined how family type contributes to the mental status of a sample of poor African-American urban children concurrently in first grade and predictively to third grade. They report that: (1) mother-alone families are at highest risk; (2) an absent father is less important than the aloneness of the mother; and (3) the presence of alternative adults has important ameliorative functions almost as supportive as intact mother/father family constellations. Colletta (1981) similarly notes the positive effects of alternative caregivers, reporting that mothers are more likely to reject their preschool children when they are unable to break continuous contact.

Risk Status Associated with Raising Young Children

Many researchers report that women who are poor and raising young children are at significantly greater risk of becoming depressed in comparison to other women (Brown, Bhrolchain, & Harris, 1975; Pearlin & Johnson, 1977; Radloff, 1975). The younger the mother at the birth of her first child, the greater her vulnerability to depression (McGee, Williams, & Kaskani, 1983).

Risk Associated with Large Family Size

Werner and Smith (1982) report that children are more at risk if there are four or more children in the family and if the children are spaced less than two years apart. Children from large families are most at risk due to competition for attention and lack of resources. Such children are forced to share a mother who is already highly stressed. In a family living in poverty with four or more children, the children are at twice as much risk for child abuse, due to the intensity of the parenting responsibilities and the lack of alternative coping strategies (Gil, 1970).

Risk Status Associated with Racial Minority Status

African-American families carry a multigenerational history of victimization by poverty, racism, and oppression. The high incidence of poverty among African-American children is due mainly to the high rate of female-headed households and lower earnings of African-American men.

African-American families carry a disproportionate share of the burden of poverty as a result of having less education, training, and the barriers of institutional and personalized racism. The race disparity is reflected in the following statistics: African-Americans are more likely than whites to live in families that are eligible for AFDC and to be headed by women or an unemployed or disabled man (Amott, 1990; McChesney, 1991); to have children placed in foster care, group homes, or institutions, and for a longer amount of time than non-African-Americans (Jenkins & Diamond, 1985; Taylor, Chatters, Tucker, & Lewis, 1991); to be the victim of a homicide or to die young (Amott, 1990); to be arrested, convicted, and sentenced (Amott, 1990); to be unemployed or underemployed (Buss & Redburn, 1983; McChesney, 1991; McLoyd, 1990; Taylor et al., 1991; Wilson & Neckerman, 1986); and for an adolescent to give birth outside of marriage (Furstenberg & Brooks-Gunn, 1987).

Several researchers have reported that African-American families are more likely than other families to suffer from long-term poverty (Duncan & Rodgers, 1988; Ellwood, 1988; McLoyd, 1990; Wilson & Neckerman, 1986). These inequalities wear African-American families down and undermine their coping abilities (Clark, 1983). Resignation, fatalism, or increased violence are common responses to the injustices they feel.

The high rate of female-headed families living in poverty is largely due to the precarious economic situation of African-American men (Center for the Study of Social Policy, 1986; Garfinkel & McLanahan, 1986; Staples, 1986; Wilson & Neckerman, 1986). African-American women have a very small pool of economically stable men to choose from who have enough money to support a family (Amott, 1990; Staples, 1986). Due to this financial situation of African-American men, marital relationships are undermined (Amott, 1990; Bishop, 1977; Staples, 1986), and there is an increased risk of family violence (McLoyd, 1990).

It has been noted that when African-American men contribute even meager amounts toward child support, this is highly appreciated by the women (Stack, 1970). It was reported in one study that child-support and alimony payments accounted for only 3.5% of income to single African-American mothers (McLanahan & Booth, 1989). Not surprisingly, Dressler (1985) reports that chronic economic stress is the strongest predictor of depression among African-Americans.

History of Trauma, Loss, and Victimization

Research shows that a significant number of homeless women have experienced multiple losses, victimization, trauma, and instability in their childhood and adult lives. Some researchers suggest that these conditions leave women particularly vulnerable to becoming homeless in the first place (Bassuk, Rubin, & Lauriat, 1986; Browne, 1993; Hagen, 1987).

Such traumatic experiences can result in: disaffiliation from family members as a protective network (Fulmer, 1987; Hausman & Hammen, 1993; McChesney, 1988); difficulty trusting others, which can result in isolation and an inability to develop intimate relationships (Anthony, 1987; Browne, 1993; Herman & Hirschman, 1977; Walker, 1979); an inability to cope with the developmental tasks of parenthood (Egeland & Kreutzer, 1991; Finkelhor & Browne, 1985; Herman, 1992); low self-esteem (Brown & Harris, 1978; Wright, 1982); a vulnerability to repeating abuse with their own children (Herrenkohl, Herrenkohl, & Toedter, 1983); a vulnerability to further victimization (Browne, 1993; Walker, 1983); an increased sense of helplessness and hopelessness because of lost belief in their own actions having an impact (Seligman, 1975); a greater vulnerability to turning to drugs as a coping strategy (Burnam et al., 1988; Weinreb & Bassuk, 1990); and long-term psychological impairment (Brown & Ziefert, 1990).

Early events in these women's lives may modify their sensitivities to stress or coping abilities, predisposing them to disorders from stressful life events (Rutter, 1983). Based on the work of Brown and Harris (1978), Fulmer (1987) states, "Accumulation of past losses and current stress factors engender a feeling of hopelessness that makes the impact of current loss much greater" (p. 25). Brown and Ziefert (1990) add, "The losses associated with their homelessness are merely repetitions of the many losses of their earlier lives" (p. 11).

Several researchers have put forth the idea that past losses sensitize an individual and make it more difficult for them to deal with new losses. Gunnar et al. (1989) assert that a vulnerability to homelessness may be linked to a lack of a trusting secure attachment in childhood, which serves as the "roots of coping" (Ainsworth, 1982; Bowlby, 1969; Mahler, Pine, & Bergman, 1975; Sandler, 1975).

Janoff-Bulman and Frieze (1983) assert that trauma victims "no longer perceive themselves as safe and secure in a benign environment [because] they have experienced a malevolent world (p. 5). These authors assert that "feelings of intense anxiety and helplessness accompany the victim's lost sense of safety" (p. 4) The end result is that trauma victims "perceive themselves as powerless and helpless in the face of forces beyond their control" (p. 6).

The loss of secure bonds or the inability to ever form a secure relationship impacts on self-esteem, self-reliance, and a basic trust in the world. Early experiences can be very influential in determining the extent to which an individual will persevere in the face of current stressors. If people feel that they have no control over events or other persons in their lives and that situations exceed their coping abilities, they will come to believe that outcomes are independent of their actions. This attitude will leave them more prone to surrendering in the face of adversity.

Seligman (1975) explains that "learned helplessness" produces fear and then depression. He states, "The depressed patient believes or has learned that he cannot control those elements of his life that relieve suffering, bring gratification, or provide nurture—in short, he believes that he is helpless" (p. 93).

Homeless women are at great risk of depression and learned helplessness because they are forced to contend with environmental forces over which they have little control, they are exposed to repeated victimization that increases their sense of helplessness and hopelessness, and they have few alternatives (Walker, 1979).

Children whose mothers have grown up in poverty are at greater risk because of their long-term exposure to oppressive conditions over which they have had little control. This state of helplessness can be transmitted cross-generationally. Homelessness is yet another experience of deprivation that is likely to increase depressed feelings that were present before (Goodman, Saxe, & Harvey, 1991).

The Prevalence of Childhood Abuse in Homeless Mothers' Lives

High rates of childhood sexual and physical abuse, ranging from 31% to 60%, have been reported by many researchers (Bassuk & Rosenberg, 1988; Browne, 1993; D'Ercole & Struening, 1990; Goodman, 1991a; Redmond & Brackmann, 1990; Rog, McCombs-Thorton, Gilbert-Mongelli, Brito & Holupka, 1995; Shinn, Knickman, & Weitzman, 1991; Vostanis, Grattan, Cumella, & Winchester, 1997; Wood, Valdez, Hayashi, & Shen, 1990).

Bassuk and Rosenberg (1988) reported that at least 42% of the homeless women in their sample had been physically abused in childhood. Wood et al. (1990) reported that 31% of the homeless women in their sample experienced physical or sexual abuse as children. Even higher numbers were reported by Redmond and

Brackmann (1990) who state that 50% of their sample of homeless women were physically abused as children, and 33% were sexually abused.

Vostanis et al. (1997) assert that the most significant characteristic of the previous histories of the 113 homeless mothers they studied was the high rate of sexual abuse (45%). Goodman (1991a) similarly reports a high rate of childhood sexual abuse. She identified that 60% of the participants in her study had a history of childhood physical abuse while 42% disclosed a history of childhood sexual abuse.

Shinn et al. (1991) reported from their large sample of homeless versus housed women in New York City that twice as many homeless as housed women disclosed childhood histories of physical and sexual abuse. In all, women requesting shelter reported higher frequencies of response on all of their six traumatic child experiences questions in comparison to the low-income housed women.

Related to these high rates of abuse found in the histories of homeless women are high rates of placement in foster care or institutional settings (Crystal, 1984). Goodman (1991a) reports that homeless women are four times more likely to have been foster children than poor housed women.

The Impact of Mother's Childhood Trauma on her Parenting

Parents are shaped by their own upbringing and experiences in childhood. They are likely to care for their children in ways that are similar to how they themselves were brought up. While there is a great propensity to repeat the past, it is not inevitable (Rutter, 1978).

Fraiberg, Adelson, and Shapiro (1980) assert that ghosts of unresolved childhood conflicts create vulnerabilities in current parenting. In one of their case examples, Fraiberg et al. surmise that the mother's nonresponsiveness to her baby's cries were the result of the fact that her own cries had never been heard. They state that the mother "closed the door on the weeping child within herself as surely as she had closed the door upon her crying baby" (p. 172).

Main and Goldwyn (1984) similarly assert that a mother's caregiving is formed from her own working model of attachment relationships. In other words, the mother's mental representation of her own childhood experience and attachment security will, to some extent, be repeated with her own child (Main, Kaplan, & Cassidy, 1985; Ricks, 1985). In this sense, mothers burdened by their own traumatic histories are at risk of repeating with their own children the traumas they themselves have suffered. They are not able to give what they have not received. While all clinicians in this area are careful to state that "history is not destiny," there is clearly a vulnerability.

If a mother was reared in poverty by a mother who was emotionally depleted, had very few resources, and received little nurturing, it will be difficult for her to give to her own child. Stiver (1990a) states, "Because these parents have so little tolerance for their own experience, they often cannot effectively allow children to convey their experience in general; and, in particular, they cannot take in the children's responses to what they see and feel in them" (p. 9).

For these parents, affects have been dissociated from experience, and not until these become reintegrated can they respond fully to their child's feelings and experience. Because these mothers were cut off at an early age from connection to their own needs, they have little understanding of their children's needs. Therefore, they may disconnect from their children, feeling incapable of meeting their needs or believe that the children are undeserving of additional care.

Stiver (1990a) states that "children are left with feelings of helplessness because they do not believe they can have an impact on their parents; they cannot participate in a mutually evolving interaction" (p. 9). Children are left with the sense that others will not want to know who they are. As the capacity for empathy was blocked in the mother, it is now blocked in the child as well. The result of this is that part of the child's self will become walled off and unavailable to him or her, resulting in a constricted emotional life and a negative image of self and others (Jordan, 1987; Miller, 1988; Stiver, 1990).

The consequences of not feeling heard or responded to leads to a sense of powerlessness, an erosion of trust, and an impaired capacity for empathy (Stiver, 1990). These are the root feelings connected with a sense of learned helplessness. Even as a young child, one can have the sense that one cannot have an effect on important people in one's life.

Low achievers in Clark's (1983) study of high-versus low-achieving poor African-American children had mothers who had been scarred by life experiences and who were working through traumas of their own childhoods. The mothers were not only depressed but also felt powerless, which led to inconsistent parenting, erratic setting of limits, and a more negative view of their children.

Several researchers have reported that parents who were abused as children were more likely to abuse their own children (Gelles, 1973;

Gil, 1971; Kempe & Helfer, 1972). These parents may lack alternative models, or their damaged self-esteem may be related to their reliance on abusive techniques. Herrenkohl et al. (1983) found that the greater the number of stresses on the family as the parent grew up, the more severe the discipline.

The devastating effects of abuse are not only the shame and humiliation it causes, but the tendency for children to blame themselves for provoking the abuse and then perceive themselves as bad, undeserving of love, and uncontrollable (Finkelhor, 1983). This is particularly true for children under the age of eight. Due to their level of cognitive development, they tend to interpret most events in relation to the self.

Mothers' Experiences of Adult Victimization and Trauma

Several researchers have identified very high rates of domestic violence in homeless samples (Anderson, Boe, & Smith, 1988; Browne, 1993; Buckner, Bassuk & Zima, 1993; Hagen & Ivanoff, 1988; Mihaly, 1991; Mills & Ota, 1989; Redmond & Brackmann, 1990; Wood et al., 1990) and assert that domestic violence is a common precipitant of homelessness.

Rog et al. (1995) reported from their large scale study of homeless families at sites in nine metropolitan communities that 81% of the women disclosed some type of abuse by a former partner.

Goodman, Saxe, and Harvey (1991) reported that 67% of their sample of homeless women had suffered some form of adult physical abuse. D'Ercole and Struening (1990) reported that 46% of their sample of homeless women had been battered, 43% raped, and 38% attacked with a weapon. They state, "We found sizable differences between groups, indicating that women in the shelters experience sexual and physical victimization at a much higher rate than do women in the urban Black population" (p. 145). Bassuk and Rosenberg (1988) similarly reported that 41% of the homeless women in their sample had been battered in at least one adult relationship, as opposed to 20% of the housed poor comparison group.

Vostanis et al. (1997) reported that one of the differences between the homeless women and the housed poor women they studied was the prevalence of domestic violence. While 37.6% of the homeless women reported a history of domestic violence, 90% of the housed women with a partner described their relationship as "supportive" and "confiding."

Mental Health Status of Homeless Women

High rates of depression, hospitalization, substance abuse, and psychological disorders caused by exposure to traumatic conditions have been reported in the literature on homeless women. Zima, Wells, Benjamin & Duan (1996) reported that 72% of the homeless mothers residing in shelters in Los Angeles County who participated in their study reported either significant current psychological distress or symptoms of a probable lifetime major mental illness or substance abuse disorder.

Rog et al. (1995) reported from their large scale study that 26% of the participants reported a serious emotional or mental health problem and 60% scored at or above the cutoff for clinical depression on the Center for Epidemiologic Depression Scale. In addition, 28% reported having made a suicide attempt, 58% of these reported having made multiple suicide attempts. These researchers identified mental health services as the greatest need for their participants across all nine sites. Similarly, Bassuk, Rubin, and Lauriat (1984) stated that as many as 90% of the women in their sample of shelter occupants were assessed as needing mental health treatment.

Zima et al. (1996) reported that homeless mothers have a higher rate of mental health problems than poor housed women yet mental health utilization is much lower. They further reported that in comparison to poor housed women, homeless mothers were almost five times as likely to abuse alcohol and three times as likely to have a drug abuse problem during the preceding 12 months.

D'Ercole & Struening (1990) reported that the women in their shelter sample were highly depressed. They found in their sample of homeless women in New York City that the mean score for the group on the Center for Epidemiologic Studies Depression Scale-Revised was 19.4, which was 10.8 points above the mean score of respondents in the community and 3.4 points above the cutoff level for clinical depression used by Weissman, Sholomskas, Pottenger, Prusoff, and Locke (1977). These researchers also noted a significant relationship between lifetime victimization and depressive symptoms. Similarly, Vostanis et al. (1997) found in their study that a mother's current psychological stress was best predicted by her previous history of victimization.

Browne (1993) also cites the high incidence of victimization in the lives of homeless women and elaborates on the relationship between survivor status and trauma symptoms.

Smith (1991) reported that 53% of a sample of 300 randomly selected homeless women in St. Louis, Missouri, met the criteria for Post-Traumatic Stress Disorder (PTSD), a condition that is defined by the inclusion of at least some of the following symptoms: numbing of responsiveness; reduced involvement with the external world; feelings of detachment and estrangement from others; constricted affect; and reexperiencing of event.

Goodman, Saxe and Harvey (1991) point out that PTSD among homeless women can be a result of trauma occurring previous to the loss of permanent housing or a response to the stressors related to losing one's home. Browne (1993) emphasizes the need for routine mental health screenings of homeless women. She states, "It is imperative that trauma histories be recognized and validated" (p.381).

The Impact of Mother's Current Mental Health Status on her Parenting

There is a large body of literature attesting to the impact of parental mental health on children's developmental and psychological functioning (Fraiberg, Adelson, & Shapiro, 1980; Hammen, 1991; Lyons-Ruth, Botein, & Grunebaum, 1984; McLoyd & Wilson, 1990; Rolf, 1972). Not surprisingly, the combined effects of mental illness and low socioeconomic status produce the worst child outcomes (Sameroff & Seifer, 1990).

Molnar and Rubin (1991) concluded from their research on poverty that homeless children's psychological development is mediated by parental distress and its subsequent effects on parenting behavior. Children can be passively affected by a withdrawn, unavailable parent or by events such as parents' life stress and lack of social support (Crnic, Greenberg, Robinson, & Ragozin, 1984; Cummings, Zahn-Waxler, & Radke-Yarrow, 1981; Thompson, Lamb, & Estes, 1982) or actively affected by parents' punitive or intrusive behavior (Sameroff & Seifer, 1983).

Several studies have identified a strong relationship between the mental health status of homeless mothers and their children. A child is at much greater risk for emotional problems if his or her mother has a mental disorder. In one study, a mother's psychiatric distress was the best predictor of behavior problems in her child (Vostanis et al., 1977). In another study, homeless school-aged children were almost four times more likely to have a behavior problem if their mother's received positive scores for lifetime major depression and three times more likely to be depressed, anxious, or withdrawn if their mother had a history of depressive symptoms (Zima et al., 1996).

Hall and Maza (1990) reported that social workers in their study observed that "children were mirroring the attitudes of their parent[s] toward the situation. Those adults who were desperately anxious about their homeless dilemma had with them children who were anxious, desperate, and difficult to manage. As adults became more resigned into homelessness and depressed, so were their children" (pp. 39-40).

Hammen (1991) reported that the children she studied were highly aware of their mother's depressed state. The more cognizant the children were, the more they tended to experience symptoms of depression.

Similarly, McLoyd and Wilson (1990) cite the work of Downey and Coyne (1990), who identified affective and behavioral differences between children of depressed and nondepressed mothers and concluded that there is a "tendency of children to imitate negative affect modeled by their mothers" (p. 52). Children of single-parent families are at greatest risk of modeling depressive affect. This is because they lack another parent who may have a more optimistic style of coping (McLoyd & Wilson, 1990).

Hughes, Parkinson, and Vargo (1987) also reported from their sample of shelter children that there was a relationship between children's anxiety levels and their mothers' anxiety levels. Anthony (1974) cites Sullivan (1953) in postulating that a fear-like state can be induced in an infant either by trauma or by contact with an emotionally disturbed mother. He states, "Her anxiety could induce anxiety in the infant through the interpersonal process of empathy" (p. 6). Anthony (1974) also cites Erikson (1950), who theorized that basic mistrust in an infant's experience was "the essence of all subsequent vulnerabilities" (p. 6).

Children's sense of security suffers when their mothers are depressed. McLoyd (1990) states, "Rewarding, explaining, consulting, and negotiating with the child require patience and concentration— qualities typically in short supply when parents feel harassed and overburdened" (p. 322). Low involvement and the use of punitive disciplinary techniques set up a cycle of negative parent-child interactions (Hammen, 1991).

McLoyd (1990) cites Longfellow, Zelkowitz, and Saunders (1982), when she stated that "among the hardest things [for mothers] to do when feeling depressed [is to be] nurturant, patient, and involved with their children" (p. 328). Again, citing Longfellow et al.'s study of five-to seven-year-old children of poor African-American and white mothers, McLoyd stated "the more depressed the mothers were, the less responsive they were to their children's dependency needs and the more likely they were to be hostile and dominating" (p. 327).

Hammen (1991) states that depressed mothers are less likely to express praise and support. Due to the mother's own level of distress, she can discount her child's need for comfort and support (George & Solomon, 1989).

Psychologically distressed low-income mothers perceive their parenting as more difficult (McLoyd, 1990) and have a tendency to perceive their children's behavior as more deviant (Christensen, Phillips, Glasgow, & Johnson, 1983; Forehand, Wells, McMahon, Griest, & Rodgers, 1982; Griest, Forehand, Wells, & McMahon, 1980; Rickard, Forehand, Wells, Griest, & McMahon, 1981).

Several researchers have reported a significant relationship between mothers' level of personal distress and their negative perceptions of children's behavior (Christensen et al., 1983; Estroff et al., 1986; Ferguson, Horwood, Gretten, & Shannon, 1985; Forehand et al., 1982; Friedlander, Weiss, & Traylor, 1986; Griest, Wells, & Forehand, 1979; Masten, Miliotis, Graham-Bermann, Ramirez, & Neeman, 1993; Schaughency & Lahey, 1985). Brody and Forehand (1986) commented that this trend fits with the theory of depression whereby depressed individuals are more pessimistic than nondepressed individuals and have lower thresholds of tolerance (Beck, Rush, Shaw, & Emery, 1979).

McLoyd and Wilson (1990) reported that mothers who experienced more negative emotional states not only perceived their parenting roles as more difficult than mothers reporting less psychological distress, but were also significantly less nurturant of their children and more communicative of their own problems. They were, for instance, more likely to talk about personal problems and the family's financial situation. Children's level of psychological distress rose in association with being placed in a parental role.

Sometimes children assume roles more similar to confidante or partner, which interferes with their own emotional development. Bassuk and Rosenberg (1988) discovered that homeless women often report their children as a source of support. When children assume parental roles, states Stiver (1990a), "the burden of responsibility which the children assume for the well-being of the parent overrides the children's own entitlement to care and devotion" (p. 9).

Zelkowitz (1982) also reports that mothers who are extremely stressed, anxious, or depressed make greater maturity demands on their children. The children were given more responsibility in running the household and assisting in tasks, while, at the same time, the mothers were less tolerant of their children's attempts to gain attention.

If a mother is using drugs as a "distraction from her hopelessness and pain" (Nyamathi & Vasquez, 1989), this will certainly impact on her children. Howard, Beckwith, Rodning, and Kropenske (1989) state, "Parents who are addicted to drugs have a primary commitment to chemicals, not to their children" (p. 8). Nyamathi and Vasquez (1989) state that many women in their study reported that "drugs became their social support" (p. 306). These researchers also cite one woman as stating, "My only friend at the time I was involved with drugs was drugs. I couldn't care less if I had a close friend or if I was close to my family" (p. 306).

PROTECTIVE FACTORS

Mother's Resiliency: Competency and Coping Behaviors

A large segment of the literature on children's resilience notes maternal competence as an important protective factor. Neiman (1988) states, "Resilient mothers . . . may provide role models of good coping skills for their children and may be more available for their children's emotional needs" (p. 24).

Educational level has been identified as an important aspect of competence. Franklin (1988) cites several studies which have concluded that "mothers who have more education value education more and communicate to their children the importance of education" (p. 270). Education can affect coping behavior through its effect on self-esteem and mastery (Milburn & D'Ercole, 1991).

O'Dougherty and Wright (1989) reported that the most consistent predictors of children's later cognitive competence are maternal education and socioeconomic status. Broman, Nichols, and Kennedy (1975) similarly reported that socioeconomic status and mother's education are two of the most predictive variables of children's intelligence scores. Masten (1989) also found that children with higher IQ scores tended to have parents who were better educated in addition to being more resourceful. Sameroff and Seifer (1983), furthermore, cite research by Bee et al. (1982), who "suggest that mothers with less education may be less able to 'buffer' the child when there are high levels of stressful life events and low levels of social support" (p. 1265).

Bronfenbrenner and Crouter (1982) state that "daughters from families in which the mother worked tended to admire their mothers more, had a more positive conception of the female role, and were more likely to be independent" (pp. 51-52). There are mixed reports on the effects of maternal employment on sons' competence.

The protective influence of maternal employment is highlighted in a study conducted by Brown, Bhrolchain, and Harris (1975). They reported that women who had a child at home, were experiencing a stressor, and did not have an intimate tie with their husbands were at much more risk of becoming emotionally disturbed if they were unemployed. When these researchers compared unemployed as opposed to employed women, 79% versus 14% became disturbed, respectively.

Anthony (1987) asserts that identification with a resilient caregiver is a critical factor. He states, "The parental egos play a crucial role in structuring the child's ego" (p. 18). "Quite typically," he writes, "'good copers' also had parents who were models of resilience themselves and who were available, but not obtrusively so, with encouragement and comforting reassurance. The parents who coped well were able to help their children to understand the problems confronting them, to work through losses sustained, and to help with restitution and compensation" (pp. 16-17).

In a similar vein, Garbarino, Kostelny, and Dubrow (1991) state, "Children will continue to cope with difficult environments and maintain reservoirs of resilience as long as parents are not pushed beyond their stress-absorption capacity . . . , [after which] the development of young children deteriorates rapidly and markedly" (p. 380).

Coping can also be understood as an active attempt made on an individual's part to modify or improve a stressful situation. By taking an active stance, one can take strides to deal with the stressful circumstances (Pearlin, Lieberman, Menaghan, & Mullan, 1981). This response set of reacting to stress and trauma with increased activity, as opposed to resigning oneself to defeat, presupposes that one has a cognitive set that, according to Seligman (1975, 1978), includes: (1) anticipating positive outcomes; (2) perceiving outcomes as within one's control; and (3) attributing failures to behaviors that can be changed. There is a cognitive set of confidence and a sense that one is in control of his or her destiny. The sense of inner control leads people to believe that they can improve their situation if only they exert an effort. These individuals are more likely to respond to crises with increased activity, to actively draw on inner and outer resources (Anthony, 1987), and therefore to model effective coping strategies for their children.

McLoyd and Wilson (1990) assert that mothers who adopt a more active stance via their situation, even though they may still be quite depressed and anxious themselves, "are more likely to be perceived by their children as competent and concerned, and . . . this may, in turn, engender a sense of efficacy and psychological security in the child" (p. 64).

Egeland and Kreutzer (1991), commenting on the work of Pianta, Egeland, and Sroufe (1990), state, "Mothers who were able to communicate positive attitudes and expectations to their child protected their child from stress, whereas mothers who communicated an attitude of pessimism, doom, and despair exacerbated the negative effects of stress" (p. 79).

Structured family routines have been associated with superior performance of preschool children in adapting to the preschool environment (Keltner, 1990). The quality of home environment has been identified as one of the most powerful predictors of developmental outcomes. An organized physical environment, appropriate play materials, and a range of stimulating activities can be very beneficial to the development of competence.

A number of researchers have emphasized the importance of support, but also the need for firm and consistent discipline. Children raised with clear structure and limits perform better academically and emotionally than those whose parents resort to punitive, erratic, and power-assertive measures (Clark, 1983; Garmezy, Masten, & Tellegen, 1984; Nuechterlein, 1970; Werner & Smith, 1982).

Clark (1983) reported from his study of high-achieving as opposed to low-achieving African-American children that it was the mothers' strength, firmness, watchful eye, and guidance that aided in their children's accomplishments. He states, "Parents have been instrumental in shaping the personality by actively catering to the child's need for emotional support, approval, reassurance, and other psychological resources" (p. 116). He describes parents of high-achieving children as speaking "supportively of the child as capable, competent, and basically healthy in mind, body, and spirit" (p. 116).

Clark goes on to state that the parents had a hopeful attitude and a belief that their children's needs would be provided for. They had a strong sense of working to improve their situation and harbored a belief that things would in fact get better. These parents were also able to handle what meager resources they had, maintained a strong sense of self-reliance, deep self-pride, and personal integrity, and saw adult kin as essential to their functioning. In sum, Clark (1983) states, "Although life in society had handed these parents a series of psychological and emotional bumps and bruises, they had basically managed with the support and encouragement of kin and friends to maintain a sense of emotional calm and rationality" (p. 116).

Factors Associated with Resilience in Children

Being the oldest child may allow for a more secure attachment to mother and more individual time with parents without having to share them with other siblings (Neiman, 1988). Taking care of siblings and being involved in what Rachman (1979) terms "required helpfulness" may provide experiences that allow for success and mastery.

Resilient children have been found to have higher levels of empathy, which are developed in positive relationships with others. They also have social problem-solving skills and coping strategies (Parker, Cowen, Work, & Wyman, 1990, as cited in Luthar & Zigler, 1991). Superior scholastic abilities have additionally been reported to have a protective effect against psychiatric disorder, even when the family is living under a great deal of chronic adversity (Rutter, 1979).

Rutter (1985) outlines characteristics associated with resilience in children. These characteristics include, in addition to an action orientation: "Firstly, a sense of self-esteem and self-confidence; secondly, a belief in one's own self-efficacy and ability to deal with change and adaption; and thirdly, a repertoire of social problem-solving approaches" (p. 607). Rutter emphasizes the importance of secure, stable interpersonal relationships and experiences of success and mastery in aiding in the above characteristics. Distancing from unalterably bad situations is also a sign of resiliency. This may include emotionally distancing from a seriously depressed, anxious, or substance-abusing parent.

Social Support

Social Networks of the Homeless

Lack of friends and family to turn to for assistance has been identified in the literature as a factor that places poor families at risk for homelessness. McChesney (1987) concludes from her research that social networks operate as a safety net to keep poor families from becoming homeless in the first place. Baumann and Grigsby (1988) similarly assert that weak family ties make families susceptible to homelessness, citing lack of both psychological support and instrumental support as key variables. Friends are identified as an important safety net should family be nonexistent.

Bassuk and Rosenberg (1988) identify strength of support network as a key variable in comparing a sample of poor housed women with homeless families. When asked to name three individuals in their personal support network to whom they could turn in times of stress, only 26% of the homeless could do so, compared to 74% of the housed mothers. Furthermore, 31% of the homeless mothers named a minor child as their only support.

Browne (1993) points to the high rates of childhood physical and sexual abuse and of domestic violence in the life histories of homeless women as an explanation for their small social support networks. Not only have these women been estranged from family members, relatives and past acquaintances as a result of their victimization, but their resultant shattered trust and suspiciousness about others' motives has kept them from seeking out or entering into new relationships.

Many researchers have reported that homeless people have small social networks and lack close ties to family and friends (Fischer, 1984; Grigsby, Baumann, Gregorich, & Roberts-Gray, 1990; McChesney, 1987; Mowbray, Solarz, Johnson, Phillips-Smith, & Combs, 1986; Rossi, Wright, Fischer, & Willis, 1987; Sosin, Colson, & Grossman, 1988; Zima et al., 1996).

In contrast, a few recent studies conducted by Goodman (1991b), Molnar, Rath, Klein, Lowe, and Hartmann (1991), and Shinn, Knickman, and Weitzman (1991) report that homeless women, compared to housed families, either have social networks similar in size and amount of support or even more social ties.

Shinn et al. (1991) reported that women seeking shelter were actually closer to their friends and family than were women in a housed comparison group. A greater number of homeless women had a living mother or grandmother, another close relative, and a close friend, and they had seen these people more recently. More than three-fourths of the homeless families had stayed with some member of their network in the past year, and more than a third had received help with their rent before becoming homeless. At the time of seeking shelter, however, the homeless women had perceived themselves as less able, in comparison to the housed sample, to stay with any of their friends or family. Shinn et al. (1991) conclude that this is evidence that resources and "social support can be used up" (p. 1184). Several of these women had been asked to leave by network members prior to seeking shelter.

Another important finding of Shinn et al.'s (1991) study is that women seeking shelter had been subjected to more disruptive early family relationships. The authors hypothesize that family ties may have been weakened early in life, leaving these women vulnerable. Weinreb and Bassuk (1990) note that personal tensions between family members can precipitate homelessness.

Definition of Social Support

A social support system consists of individuals who provide both expressive (affective) and instrumental (material) assistance. Network members may be liked or disliked and may derive from formal (community groups, professionals, service providers) or informal (family, friends, relatives) networks. Interactions can range from nurturing, supportive, and consoling to innocuous, destructive, and abusive.

Lindblad-Goldberg (1987) outlines the structural features of networks as consisting of size of network, connectiveness between members of network, and the composition of people who make up the network. Functional features include: affective exchange; informational and instrumental exchange; and reciprocity.

Social networks have special meaning in the African-American community. There is a long history of extended family networks that have served as an adaptive survival strategy developed in order to make do with limited economic resources (Malson, 1983; Stack, 1970; Taylor, Chatters, Tucker, & Lewis, 1991).

Stack (1970) reported from her research work on African-American families that goods and resources are exchanged in addition to childcare (children frequently being transferred back and forth between network members). Boyd-Franklin (1989) states, "Kinship ties make up what is perhaps one of the most enduring and important aspects of the Black African heritage" (p. 8). She explains that these ties are not necessarily drawn along blood lines. Stack (1970) uses the term "reciprocity" to describe these relationships, whereas McAdoo (1979) refers to the dynamics of "kin insurance," whereby mothers look to one another for financial assistance, childcare, advice, and emotional support.

Kinship networks and community embeddedness not only serve as an economic safety net but also as a barrier against racial oppression, which is so much a part of the social ecology of African-American families. A sense of belonging in the community, along with a group identification and African-American consciousness or pride, serves as protection to children in a racist society (Barnes, 1972). Boyd-Franklin (1989) states, "For poor, urban Black families, the task is to help motivate children to achieve and believe in themselves despite the blatant evidence of discrimination that they view every day" (p. 26). Or, in the words of Reverend Jesse Jackson, "To keep hope alive."

African-Americans' strong religious orientations (Hill, 1972; Taylor, 1988) also serve as a source of support. Black churches often function as surrogate families from whom members can get advice, help, and support (Dressler, 1985). Religious participation has been reported to buffer African-Americans against psychological distress (Brown & Gary, 1987; McLoyd, 1990).

Clark (1983) found in his study of high-achieving as opposed to low-achieving African-American children that what differentiated the former was that their families had managed to avoid "becoming victims of persistent, devastating traumas of a life-draining sort. . . . They had found mutual support groups (or individuals) within the family that soothed and comforted one another by being available for one another's day-to-day emotional and child care (and sometimes financial) needs" (p. 115).

The Dissolution of Extended Networks

Height (1985) noted that the effectiveness of the extended family network began declining several years ago, particularly among low socioeconomic families who faced burgeoning social problems. Drug addiction, for example, has served to ravage the African-American community, fragmenting support networks and creating intrafamilial disaffiliations.

When Social Ties Burden

Being a member of a social network can either enhance or inhibit family functioning. While members can bring support, they can also burden and create stress (Belle, 1982). Members can be drained of both emotional and material resources (Belle, 1983). Maya Angelou, as cited in Stack (1970), summed up the situation when she stated, "Whatever was given by Black people to other Blacks was most probably needed as desperately by the donor as by the receiver" (p. viii). The sense of obligation that members feel for one another causes them to endure sacrifices of needed resources, both psychological and material, which they may feel pressured to give away. This can lead to a feeling of being exploited and burdened by a sense of obligation (Stack, 1970; Wilson, 1986).

Lindblad-Goldberg (1987) noted in her study of poor African-American single parents that the "price of these stressful social ties may be symptomatic behavior in a family member" (p. 45). Mothers in adaptive families describe give-and-take relationships with their network members in both emotional and instrumental exchanges, whereas symptomatic families feel that they are always putting out more than they get back.

Lindblad-Goldberg and Dukes (1985) similarly reported in a comparison of African-American single mothers of dysfunctional families and African-American mothers of functional families that, despite having networks of approximately the same size, the mothers whose children were symptomatic reported that they experienced their networks as nonreciprocal. In other words, they felt that they gave more than they received. Several researchers have reported that it is not the size and availability of a social support network that is important, but the quality of functional exchange (Fulmer, 1987; Henderson, Byrne, & Duncan-Jones, 1981; Milburn & D'Ercole, 1991; Quinton, 1980).

A consistent finding in the literature of the difference between a successful and an unsuccessful social network is the perceived help or availability of help that can serve as a buffering factor in stressful situations. It is the appraisal factor and not the actual amount of help received that predicts satisfaction or dissatisfaction and impacts on family functioning (Belle, 1982; Boyd-Franklin, 1989; Taylor et al., 1991; Weinraub & Wolf, 1983; Wethington & Kessler, 1986).

Benefits of Social Support for Psychological Well-Being

The relationship between involvement in extended family support networks and improved psychological well-being has been documented in several studies (Brown & Gary, 1988; Clark, 1983; Cohen & Willis, 1985; House, Landis, & Umberson, 1988; Hughes & Demo, 1989). Social support has both direct and indirect effects on the functioning of children. Indirect effects are obtained when the mother receives emotional or instrumental support and monitoring of her parental behaviors. Children benefit from direct effects by having network members who provide support, act as role models, and provide cognitive and social stimulation.

Emotional affiliations and attachments protect individuals by buffering them from the negative effects of life events and depression. Belle (1982) reports that the extent to which poor women in her study received help with day-to-day concerns and emergencies directly impacted on their level of self-esteem and the extent to which they felt in control. She concludes that these women found basic security in help from others, which facilitated their positive mental health.

Social support has been found to be especially important when individuals are experiencing stressful circumstances (Kessler & McLeod, 1985; McLoyd, 1990; Vitaliano, Maiuro, Bolton, & Armsden, 1987). Social support has also been associated with improved parental functioning. Mothers have appeared more satisfied with their lives when they have had access to a high level of social support (Abernathy, 1973; Crnic, Greenberg, Ragozin, Robinson, & Basham, 1983). They have also felt less overwhelmed by their parenting responsibilities and happier with their children (Crnic & Greenberg, 1987; Zur-Szpiro & Longfellow, 1982). Colletta (1981) reported that emotional support was the strongest predictor of maternal behavior for a sample of African-American and white low-income adolescent mothers. Emotional support was found to be even more important than material, informational, and child-care support.

Garcia-Coll, Vohr, Hoffman, and Oh (1986) reported that mothers who felt supported were more responsive to their eight-month-old infants and less punitive to them. Crockenberg (1981) reported a relationship between social support and secure attachment in toddlers who had been irritable babies. Pascoe, Loda, Jeffries, and Earp (1981) found that mothers who were provided with more social support, regardless of stress level, were more stimulating to their three-year-old children. Crockenberg (1987) reported from a sample of low income adolescent mothers that maternal sensitivity increased in relation to amount of help the mother received from family members. Similarly, Furstenberg and Crawford (1978) reported from their sample of predominantly African-American teen mothers that those who continued living with their families of origin had children who had less behavior problems and who scored higher on cognitive tests than the children of adolescent mothers who lived alone or with relatives.

Cotterell (1986) reported that informational support is associated with improved sensitive parenting. Mothers in her study became more involved and supportive and had a greater tolerance level for children's behaviors. Heincke, Beckwith, and Thompson (1988) reported that programs which allowed parents the opportunity to form relationships with mental health professionals had the most positive effects on family functioning.

Several studies emphasize the positive effects of additional caregivers. Thompson and Ensminger (1989) report that among the African-American women with school-aged children they studied, those who lived with a spouse or mother were less psychologically distressed than those who lived alone. Rutter (1987) reports that a spouse plays a supportive role because he or she shares in the burden of parenting. The presence of a partner or spouse has been found to be beneficial by other researchers as well (Brown & Harris, 1978; Parker & Hazdi-Pavlovic, 1984). Zur-Szpiro and Longfellow (1982) report that fathers' support decreased depression among women and had the effect of causing the children to view their fathers' as more nurturant.

Even though there are benefits to a two-parent household, societal barriers such as attaining welfare entitlements and high unemployment rates discourage fathers' presence in the home. Diamant (1986) reported from her interview with Stanley F. Battle that African-American fathers are concerned about their children, but feel they have little to offer them.

Myers (1982) noted that single parents are "frequently not alone" (p. 56) and observed that fathers can be companions who move in and out of the home. Several researchers have noted that the father-child relationship is largely dependent on the relationship between the mother and father and the mother's attitude toward the father (Bronfenbrenner, 1986; Elder, 1974, 1979; McLoyd, 1990).

While Brown and Harris (1978) noted a mother's depression when she lacked a relationship with a boyfriend or husband, several researchers emphasize the quality of the relationship and not simply the presence of a partner that improves the mother's mental health status (Fulmer, 1987). Hetherington (1980) similarly asserts that it is better for a child to have one parent than two if the other parent is hostile and rejecting. This position is consistent with other research that emphasizes that it is the quality and not the quantity of members in one's support network that is important (Lindblad-Goldberg & Dukes, 1985).

Bernard (1966) found in her study of low-income families that fathers participated very little in child-rearing duties and that in some instances the absence of the father results in little loss because he is not a positive model. Ball (1986) explained that African American womens' satisfaction with having a husband can be attributed to exchange theory where, according to Staples (1986), "the costs of such an arrangement [may] outweigh the benefits" p.28.

Research that shows the more direct influence of support on children's functioning comes from Sandler, Miller, Short, and Wolchik (1989). They report that support aids in children's psychological adjustment and protects them from the negative effects of stressful experiences. When a parent is psychologically unavailable, the presence of others, such as grandparents, siblings, neighbors, or day-care providers, gains importance because of the role they can play in compensating for the absent parent (Werner & Smith, 1982).

Rutter (1990) reported that one good relationship with a parent can have a substantial protective effect on a child who otherwise lives in a discordant, unhappy home. The presence of a father in the home for boys plays an important protective role and has been reported to be a significant predictor of resiliency (Werner & Smith, 1982).

Network members can also serve an important role in cognitive and social stimulation of children (Cochran & Brassard, 1979). Greater network support to children, particularly under high stress, has been related to significantly fewer behavior problems, as compared to those children who received low social support (O'Grady & Metz, 1987).

Williams and Kornblum (1985) report from their study of poor African-American urban children that an adult who could serve as a positive role model, who demonstrated an interest in the child, and who sheltered them to some extent from their neighborhoods was a significant aspect in what they termed "superkids."

Several studies have documented that resilient children will seek out relationships and reach out to others outside the family for support.

These children seem particularly adept at drawing in substitute caregivers, surrogate parents, and role models to help them during times of crisis (Murphy & Moriarty, 1976; Pines, 1979; Werner, 1984). Werner and Smith (1982), as cited by McLoyd and Wilson (1990), reported that all the high-risk resilient children in their study had recruited a mentor at some time in their lives to help them through. They stated, "Many of these children had very early memories of a special adult who fostered confidence in their ability to succeed in spite of obstacles" (p. 54).

Older siblings are an important support resource to moderate effects of stress on younger children. They can reduce exposure to stressors and aid in the social and cognitive development of younger siblings (Cicirelli, 1976; Jaffe, Wolfe, & Wilson, 1990; Lamb, 1978; Werner & Smith, 1982). Molnar et al. (1988) reported observing particularly strong sibling bonds among homeless children.

Day-care providers can be significant figures in young children's lives, and a day-care environment has been shown to have significant benefits even for children who have attended for as short a time as three months (Collins & Pancoast, 1976; Molnar et al., 1991).

Several studies show that social networks buffer the negative effects of economic hardship. For those families without access to a support system, there is a heightened risk that they will take out their frustrations on each other or their children (Cazenave & Straus, 1979; Daniel, Hampton, & Newberger, 1983; Garbarino, 1976; Gelles, 1980; Trickett & Susman, 1988).

Network members serve not only to provide support to mothers and their children but also to impose sanctions on mothers' harsh parenting behaviors. Hunter and Kilstrom (1979) report that social support is a significant factor in differentiating between which parents repeat an intergenerational cycle of child abuse and which do not. Regular church attendance has also been noted to serve a protective function against neglect (Giovannoni & Billingsley, 1970).

LITERATURE REVIEW SUMMARY AND HYPOTHESES

A review of the literature indicates that few empirical studies on homeless children exist. The data that is in suggests that an experience of homelessness can have a very damaging effect on the psychological, behavioral, and cognitive functioning of children. There are many more studies on the effects of poverty on children than ones that specifically address homelessness. It is unclear, at this time, what differentiates housed children who have experienced poverty from homeless children who have experienced poverty. We cannot assume that these are equivalent experiences.

Some of the major differences between women who live in poverty and those who have become homeless appear to be relational. Homeless women are reported to have suffered more trauma and victimization beginning at a younger age and extending into adulthood. While the literature is inconsistent in regard to size and contact with social support networks, it is generally agreed that homeless womens' social ties are often strained. In addition, it is unclear if the women's reported increased substance usage is a cause of, or response to, their homeless situation.

The literature on the parenting practices of homeless mothers has described their despair, confusion, sense of powerlessness, and, in general, "the unraveling of their mother role." It has been suggested that strong sibling bonds may serve a protective function for younger children. In general, due to the uncertainty of homeless living, children are forced to contend with a great deal of change, inconsistency, and frightening situations. These are all conditions that appear antithetical to secure attachment and the development of a sense of safety and self-esteem.

Nonetheless, some children do better than others. The literature, arguing for a cross-generational transmission of resiliency, suggests that an important factor may be the mother's own competence. Other factors that have been cited include: amount of social support and resources available to the family; mother's current psychological functioning and ability to cope; her educational and work history; the degree of losses she has endured; the number of stressful life events she has had to contend with; the composition of the family; and the child's basic constitution and health status.

In light of the literature presented on risk and protective factors operating within individuals and families, and the multiplicity of social forces involved, the researcher puts forth the following five hypotheses:

1. It is anticipated that mothers (a) who are currently in the least psychological distress (as measured by the Center for Epidemiologic Studies Depression Scale and Taylor Manifest Anxiety Scale), (b) who have achieved a high level of competent functioning (as measured by education and work

history) and (c) who have, despite enormous environmental stressors, coped at a high level (as measured by absence of chronicity of drug and alcohol addiction, presence of suicide attempts, or a history of treatment for a psychiatric condition) will be better able to model resilience and have more emotionally and behaviorally resilient children.

2. It is predicted that relational variables (e.g., separations, losses, and unavailability of mother due to drug use, depression, or domestic violence) will be more predictive of child outcomes than other variables.

3. It is anticipated that chronicity of poverty (e.g., length of time homeless, number of moves, unemployment, low education, and training) will be associated with children's emotional/behavioral and cognitive outcome.

4. It is predicted that the more social support and resources available to the family, the more resilient the children will be.

5. It is anticipated that children will be more competent if they have not suffered prenatal or perinatal health complications, if they are eldest, and if they have a fewer number of siblings. Additionally, it is expected that children with fewer stressful life events will be more resilient.

CHAPTER III
Methods

OVERVIEW

The purpose of this study was to investigate the psychological and developmental status of young children who have recently had an experience of being homeless. The major aim of the study was to identify processes and factors that may mediate negative outcomes. The intent was to identify not only the stressors in these children's lives that appeared to be most detrimental, but also the factors that appeared to be most protective and buffering in counterbalancing stress. Specifically, the hope was to understand the dynamics that lead to or contribute to resiliency in high-risk children who share a common history of homelessness.

While there is a small body of research on homeless children, the emphasis has been exclusively on what has gone wrong with the majority versus what has gone right with the few. The research emphasizes the disproportionate number of homeless children who suffer from emotional, physical, and developmental delays. Furthermore, in the data that is available, little is known about the specific factors of the homeless families' circumstances that lead to the poor outcomes. While we have limited information on the isolated specific dynamics that give rise to poor outcomes, we have no information on the characteristics that facilitate good adjustment.

The present researcher's goal in studying children who do well, despite serious stressors, was to identify factors associated with their good outcomes so that effective intervention services could be planned to reduce the risk for other children growing up under similar conditions and circumstances.

METHOD OF DATA COLLECTION

This study utilized some of the data that has been collected as part of a larger research and evaluation study conducted by The Better Homes Fund in Newton Centre, Massachusetts. The Better Homes Fund has collected data to assess the effectiveness of a service system that provides housing, a network of services, and intensive long-term case management to high-risk, multiproblem, homeless pregnant women and their families.

Family data that this researcher utilized in her study fall into the following broad areas: health and prenatal care; history of homelessness and dependence on public assistance; extent of educational and vocational attainment; mental health status; drug abuse and family violence history; legal status; support networks; and current service utilization. Child data includes health, developmental, psychological, behavioral, cognitive, and service utilization information.

While the interviews consisted of a standardized set of questions, the mothers were given an opportunity to emphasize matters of importance, reflect, make associations, and tell their story in their own way. This was done in an attempt to capture the richness and diversity of these women's lives. The women spoke from their frame of reference as African-Americans and as survivors of at least one episode of homelessness. These women, despite persistent stressors in their lives, were able to work their way off the streets with the support of program staff. This accomplishment in itself is a testament to their inner resources.

SUBJECTS

All of the participants were women and children of color, specifically African-American, reflecting both the location and the association between race and poverty in the United States. The families are participants in a enriched perinatal services program at an agency in Oakland, California and were enrolled as Better Homes Fund research subjects.

To qualify to participate in the larger study, the families must have identified themselves as Oakland residents who were currently homeless and who, in addition to lack of a home must have been pregnant upon entry and have at least one of the following conditions:

1. The mother must have a significant alcohol or drug problem; and/or

2. The mother must have a history of treatment for a chronic mental health condition, or a developmental or physical disability; and/or

3. The family must have a combination of social, educational, and other problems so severe that the family has been homeless for at least 12 of the preceding 24 months.

Of the thirty-seven women who had been interviewed at the time of this study, seventeen (47%) had preschool children and therefore met criteria for participation. Major demographic variables of the sample are presented in Tables 1, 2, and 3.

Child subjects' ages ranged from 3.0 to 6.4-years-old (mean age = 4.4 years). Eight children were male (47.1%) and nine children were female (52.9%). Six children were firstborns (35.3%), six children were second-borns (35.3%), four were third-born (23.5%), and one was fourth-born (5.9%).

The mothers of the children ages ranged from 19 to 43-years-old (mean age = 29 years). Fathers' ages ranged from 21 to 54-years-old (mean age = 35 years). The majority of the children's mothers (12) have never been married (70.6%), 3 were currently married (17.6%), and 2 were divorced (11.8%). Most mothers (15) had their high school diploma or its equivalency (88.2%), and 8 had some college or graduated from job training (47.1%). One of the women was currently employed (5.9%).

The majority of the women (10) described themselves as Baptist (58.8%), five women professed no religious affiliation (29.8%), and one family each proclaimed themselves Catholic (5.9%) and Jehovahs' Witness (5.9%).

Table 1: Sample and Descriptive Statistics (N=17)

Subject Variables	MIN	MAX	MEAN	SD
Child's Age (years)	3.0	6.4	4.42	1.14
Mother's Current Age (years)	19	43	28.71	5.74
Father's Current Age (years)	21	54	34.88	9.27
Mother's Age at Child's Birth	15	39	24.06	5.90

Table 2: Mother's Marital Status, Religious Orientation, and Number of Children Living in the Home (N=17)

Mother's Current Marital Status	n	%
Married	3	17.6
Divorced	2	11.8
Never Married	12	70.6
Religious Orientation	n	%
Baptist	10	58.8
Catholic	1	5.9
Jehovah's Witness	1	5.9
No Religious Affiliation	5	29.8
Number of Children Living in the Home	n	%
One	0	0
Two	7	41.2
Three	3	17.65
Four	4	23.5
Five or more	3	17.65

Table 3: Mother's Educational Level and Occupational Status (N=17)

Education	n	%
Licensed Professional	1	5.9
Some College or Completed Job Training	7	41.2
GED or High School Diploma	7	41.2
Less than High School	2	11.7
Previous Occupation	n	%
Professional	1	5.9
Skilled	4	23.5
Semi-Skilled	9	52.9
Unskilled	3	17.6
Highest Salary (per hour)	n	%
$9.00 +	2	11.8
$8.00 - $8.99	1	5.9
$7.00 - $7.99	4	23.5
$6.00 - $6.99	3	17.6
Less than $6.00	7	41.2
Longest Period of Employment	n	%
5 years +	2	11.8
3 - 5 years	3	17.6
1 - 3 years	3	17.6
6 - 12 years	5	29.4
Less than 6 months	4	23.5

PROCEDURE

Prospective participants were identified by service providers throughout the Enhanced Perinatal Services Network. The subjects for the study were recruited in the following way:

1. After qualifying for program services by having met the criteria outlined above, in addition to following through on some of the goals and objectives set forth by their Case Manager, families received their Section 8 certificate. The certificate subsidizes their rent for five years and allows them to pay a maximum of 30 percent of their income. After each family procured housing, the Program Assistant contacted families by telephone to explain the study. Those families who expressed an interest were then asked to give verbal consent to be called by the evaluator. Families without telephones were sent a letter explaining the nature of the study and asked to call the Program Assistant if they were interested in participating.

2. Families were then contacted by the evaluator and given additional information about the study. They were informed about the length of the interviews, number of visits, confidentiality and remuneration for their participation. Interested families were then scheduled for an Initial Family Interview.

3. During the first face-to-face contact, which generally took place in subject's homes, the limits of confidentiality were explained, the consent form was read and the opportunity to ask questions about the interviewing procedure or research project was granted. After the mother signed the consent form, the first interview was conducted. Some mothers chose to do this interview in two appointments, others completed the three hour interview in one. All families were paid $25.00 in cash after the Initial Family Interview was completed.

4. The second appointment consisted of administering the Wechsler Preschool and Primary Scale of Intelligence-Revised (WPPSI-R) to the child, asking the child to draw a person, having the mother complete the Child Behavior Checklist (CBCL) form and interviewing the mother in order to complete the Preschool Child Assessment: Initial Interview form. The

WPPSI-R takes about one hour to administer and the mother's interview and CBCL averages a half hour each.

MEASURES

Initial Family Interview

This structured interview instrument was compiled by The Better Homes Fund. It includes seven sections and takes about two-and-a-half to three-and-a-half hours to administer. Section I consists of background information and contains questions in regards to demographics, education, work history, income and entitlements, childhood family history, legal status, children, family composition and housing history. Section II contains questions about general health and includes a nutrition questionnaire. Section III contains questions about mother's service utilization during the past three months. Section IV includes a NIMH General Mental Health Inventory in addition to the Center for Epidemiologic Studies Depression Scale (Radloff, 1977) and Taylor Manifest Anxiety Scale (Taylor (1953). Section V covers substance (drug and alcohol) use over the past year and history of drug treatment. Section VI contains questions about childhood, adult, and current (during the past year) family violence. Included in this section is the Conflict Tactics Scale developed by Straus (1979). Section VII contains questions about support networks. It includes a Network Inventory which is a modification of PASS developed by Dunst and Trivette. This section also contains a Life Stress Inventory pertaining to the past year and a Family Resource Scale developed by Dunst, Trivette, and Deal to measure adequacy of family resources during the past year.

Preschool Child Assessment: Initial Interview

This structured interview was compiled by The Better Homes Fund. It asks questions about the child's general health, and includes the NHIS Health Conditions: Childhood Conditions questionnaire and a section on services the child has received over the past three months.

Wechsler Preschool and Primary Scale of Intelligence-Revised (WPPSI-R)

The WPPSI-R is a standardized measure of intellectual ability that is normed for children ages three years to seven years, three months. The

WPPSI-R contains 12 subtests, 6 in the Performance scale and 6 in the Verbal scale. The most appropriate process of interpretation utilizes a three level approach.

The first level, Full Scale IQ score, is the most reliable level. The data yielded is both quantitative (IQ ranges) and qualitative (standard deviations, percentiles). The second level involves comparing Verbal and Performance scale scores. A significant discrepancy between the scales yields important interpretive information regarding strengths and weaknesses. A third level of interpretation is a comparison of difference between individual subset scores and the means of the combined Verbal and combined Performance scaled scores.

The standardization sample for the WPPSI-R is representative of the 1986 U.S. census demographics. The standardization sample consisted of 15.3 percent African-American children.

The WPPSI-R has excellent reliabilities for the Performance, Verbal and Full Scale I.Q.'s. Internal consistency reliabilities are above .90. Subtest reliabilities are less satisfactory and range from .63 (Object Assembly) and .86 (Similarities).

Since the WPPSI-R is new, few studies are available in regards to its validity. It is asserted, however, that the studies relating to the validity of the WPPSI are indicative of adequate construct, concurrent and predictive validity for the WPPSI-R (Sattler 1990). Research cited in the WPPSI-R manual indicate that there are similarities between children's performance on the WISC-R, Stanford Binet Intelligence Scale-4th Edition, McCarthy Scales of Children's Abilities, K-ABC and WPPSI-R. This suggests good concurrent validity.

Child Behavior Checklist (CBCL/4-18)

The Child Behavior Checklist is a behaviorally based descriptive inventory developed by Achenbach and Edelbrock (1983) to assess children's functioning and identify children who need further psychological evaluation. The CBCL/4-18 was revised by Achenbach (1991) with new national norms (see Appendix A).

The CBCL/4-18 contains a list of 118 behavior problems and 20 social competence items. A parent is asked to rank each item on a three-point scale from 0=not true, 1=somewhat or sometimes true, to 2=very true or often true. Mothers' in this study were read the questions out loud and the researcher recorded the answers. This is an acceptable form of administration when there is uncertainty about a parent's reading level or comprehension.

Achenbach and Edelbrock (1983) factor analyzed parents' ratings of a large sample of clinically referred children separately for both genders and for each of the following age groups 4-5, 6-11, and 12-16. For each age and sex group, factors were identified which made up syndromes of problems. Children's scores on each scale can be transformed into an empirically derived syndrome. The normative data allows for comparison between same sex peers. Second order factor analyses of the syndromes allows for categorization into the broader syndrome groups which have been labelled internalizing and externalizing.

The nine separate syndrome scales include: Withdrawn; Somatic Complaints; Anxious/Depressed; Social Problems; Thought Problems; Attention Problems; Sex Problems; Delinquent Behavior; and Aggressive Behavior. An Internalizing Scale is made up of the Withdrawn, Somatic Complaints and Anxious/Depressed syndromes, while an Externalizing Scale contains the Delinquent Behavior and Aggressive Behavior Syndromes. There is a mean correlation of .52 between Internalizing and Externalizing scale scores suggesting that many children with problems exhibit both internalizing and externalizing behaviors while other children present more clearly one or the other.

The total behavior problem score is the most accurate index of a child's global functioning and has the strongest relationship to predicting clinical status. The social competence score is the least reliable predictor for differentiating between referred and nonreferred children at the 4-5 age level because school items are not scored creating a "floor effect."

The CBCL is well standardized and has adequate reliability and validity. The CBCL was found to discriminate strongly between children referred for mental health services and nonreferred children who were demographically matched (Achenbach & Edelbrock, 1983). Children referred for mental health services obtained significantly higher scores than nonreferred children on all the behavioral and emotional items as well as on the total problem score. The CBCL has accurately discriminated between many different samples of clinical and nonclinical children.

The CBCL is particularly valid cross-culturally due to the sampling procedures that were used. Achenbach and Edelbrock (1981) found in their normative sample that of the 119 items analyzed for demographic differences, only five showed significant race effects, and all of the effect sizes were small.

SES differences in reported behavior problems is larger than racial differences. Gender differences have consistently shown a trend where boys score higher on externalizing items and girls score higher on internalizing items.

Child Behavior Checklist (CBCL/2-3)

The CBCL/2-3 is a parent report measure of emotional/behavioral problems in 2-and 3-year-old children (see Appendix B). The checklist includes 99 problem items, 59 of which appear on the CBCL/4-18 form. Parents are asked to rate their child on the previous 2-month period. The CBCL/2-3 requires only a fifth-grade reading level.

The 1986 profile for scoring the CBCL/2-3 includes six syndrome scales: Social Withdrawal; Depressed; Sleep Problems; Somatic Problems; Aggressive; and Destructive. The scales were derived from principal components/varimax analyses of 398 children, including referred, nonreferred and at-risk children. Norms are based on the 273 nonreferred children who were randomly selected from the general population. Internalizing, externalizing, and total problem scores are computed similar to the CBCL/4-18. The exception is that there are not separate norms for the sexes due to no significant differences found.

Achenbach, Edelbrock, and Howell (1987) reported acceptable reliability, stability, and predictive validity for the CBCL/2-3. The mean correlations between the ages of 2 to 4 and 3 to 4 was .65 for boys and .52 for girls. Age and ethnicity were not significantly associated with any scale scores but lower SES children had significantly higher scores on most scales. Children referred for mental health services scored significantly higher than nonreferred children.

Child Behavior Rating Form

A Child Behavior Rating Form was constructed by the researcher to capture children's interactional abilities, sense of mastery, self-esteem, motivation, frustration-tolerance, and ability to use goal-oriented strategies versus resignation (See Appendix C). The form was used to collect independent observational data on the children. The researcher scored the rating form after the home visit was made where the child was tested.

The Center for Epidemiologic Studies Depression Scale(CES-D)

The CES-D is a self-report measure developed by the Center for Epidemiologic Studies to measure depressive symptomatology in the community (see Appendix D). Items were selected from five existing scales: Zung's depression scale (1965, 1967), a depression inventory developed by Beck, Ward, Mendelson, Mock, and Erbaugh (1961), a self-report scale developed by Raskin, Schulterbrandt, Reating, and McKeon (1969), items from the Minnesota Multiphasic Inventory (Dahlstrom & Welsh, 1960), and a scale developed by Gardner (1968). The CES-D was constructed specifically to assess current frequency of depressive symptoms. It is a 20 item questionnaire that assesses the frequency of symptoms over the preceding week on a 4 point scale from 0 ("rarely or

none of the time"), 1 ("some or little of the time"), 2 (occasionally or moderate amount of time"), and 3 ("most or all of the time")

The measure consists of six components: depressed mood, feelings of guilt, worthlessness, psychomotor retardation, loss of appetite, and sleep disturbance. Four items are included on the scale that are representative of nondepressed mood.

Scores range from 0 to 60, with higher scores indicating depressive symptomatology. Radloff (1977) suggested that a total score of 16, which discriminates between the upper 20 percent of the score distribution in general population studies, be used as a cutoff to indicate "case" depression. However, it has been noted (Devins & Orme, 1985) that a substantial proportion of respondents who are actually clinically depressed may obtain CES-D scores below the cutoff indicating that some false negatives will result from using the score of 16 as a criterion. Myers and Weissman (1980) and Roberts and Vernon (1983) similarly reported a false negative rate of between 36 and 40 percent in their samples when they used the cutoff score of 16.

Barnes and Prosen (1985) on the other hand, have suggested that scores below 16 indicate that the individual is "not depressed," scores from 16 to 20 indicate, "mild depression," scores from 21 to 30 indicate "moderate depression," and scores of 31 and greater indicate severe depression.

The CES-D has been shown to have similar validity among African-American, Caucasian and Hispanic respondents (Devins and Orme, 1985). In addition, Radloff (1977) has reported that the CES-D has, "discriminated well between psychiatric inpatient and general population samples and discriminated moderately among levels of severity within patient groups (p. 393)."

Barnes and Prosen (1985) and Radloff (1977) have reported internal consistency coefficients of .84 and above. Test-retest reliabilities have demonstrated to be quite consistent (Radloff 1977) and the CES-D has correlated significantly with other measures of depression (Devins and Orme, 1985; Radloff, 1977) indicating acceptable convergent validity.

Taylor Manifest Anxiety Scale (TMAS)

The Taylor Manifest Anxiety Scale (Taylor, 1953) is a 50 item true-false scale which measures clients' level and sensitivity of anxiety-related symptomatology (see Appendix E). It was developed by having judges rate 200 items from the MMPI according to how representative they were of manifest anxiety. After statistical analysis, the original 65 statements for which there was at least 80 percent agreement among the judges were reduced to 50 of the most discriminating statements.

Hilgard, Jones, and Kaplan (1951) reported a split-half reliability of .92 and Gocka (1965) an internal consistency value of .92. Taylor (1953) reported high test-retest reliability coefficients of .89 for a 3 week interval and .82 for a 5 month interval indicating that the test is psychometrically sound. The TMAS has correlated highly with other measures of anxiety. Due to the high correlations with a number of other scales, Gotlib and Cane (1989) state, "It appears that the TMAS is a trait measure that assesses a number of different dimensions relating to general negative reactivity, dissatisfaction with the self, and discomfort in social or interpersonal situations" (p. 143). O'Connor, Lorr, and Stafford (1956) reported five factors for the TMAS: chronic anxiety or worry; increased physiological activity; sleep disturbance associated with inner strain; personal inadequacy; and motor tension.

Davids (1955) as cited in Livneh and Redding (1986) asserted that the TMAS is subject to respondents attempts to present themselves in a favorable light due to the construction of the test having been based on face validity.

Conflict Tactics Scales

The Conflict Tactics Scales (CTS) was developed by Straus (1979) to measure the use of reasoning, verbal aggression and violence perpetrated by an adult male within a family (see Appendix F). The CTS contains a list of 21 actions which a male partner of a respondent may have taken to resolve conflict. They range from "discussing an issue calmly" to verbal abuse, physical abuse and the extreme of forcing sex and performing life-threatening acts. The respondent is to state the number of times for each category ranging from "never" to "more than 20 times" that their partner has used this approach with them in the past year. Physical violence items are divided into two levels of severity: minor and severe. Minor includes throwing an object, pushing, shoving, and slapping. Severe includes kicking, biting, hitting with a fist or object, beating, choking and threatening or using a knife or gun. The CTS was normed on a nationally representative sample of 2,143 couples.

Table 4: Summary of Child and Adult Measures

Child Measures
Child Behavior Checklist
Wechsler Preschool and Primary Scale of Intelligence-Revised
Projective Drawing
Child Behavior Rating Form
Adult Measures
The Center for Epidemiologic Studies Depression Scale
Taylor Manifest Anxiety Scale
Conflict Tactics Scale

DATA ANALYSIS

1. Children's cognitive resiliency was determined by utilizing the following WPPSI-R cutoff scores:

   WPPSI-R Full Scale IQ >90
   Verbal IQ >90
   Performance IQ >90

2. Children had to score in the Average range (90) on the Full Scale IQ and on both the Verbal and Performance subtests in order to be classified as cognitively competent.

3. Children's emotional/behavioral resiliency was determined by a score of $T < 60$ on the CBCL Total Behavior Problem Scale.

4. Children were then divided into two separate groups. Group 1 consisted of cognitively competent as opposed to incompetent children, and Group 2 consisted of children who were assessed to be resilient in the emotional/behavioral domain versus those who were not.

5. Each child's mother's scores on the CES-D and TMAS were then calculated. The following cutoff scores were used to differentiate those women who fell in the clinical range versus those who did not.

   CES-D < 16
   TMAS < 21

6. Women were classified as having been battered if they had in the past year been kicked, bitten, hit with a fist or object, beaten up, choked, strangled, smothered, threatened with a knife, gun, or automobile, stabbed, or shot at.

7. Children were then individually ranked on the following clusters of variables:

   a. Mother's Competence (education and employment history)
   b. Chronicity of Poverty
   c. Mother's Current Psychological Functioning (CES-D score and Taylor Manifest Anxiety score)
   d. Mother's History of Psychological Coping (psychiatric and drug abuse history)
   e. Mother's Stressful Life Events (as child/adolescent and adult)
   f. Mother's Exposure to Trauma and Victimization
   g. Child's Birth/Health Status
   h. Child's Stressful Life Events
   i. Families Natural Support Network and Resources
   j. Agency Support
   k. Child's School/Day Care Attendance

   Refer to Appendix G for a complete listing of the variables contained in each cluster.

8. Children were then compared according to their group membership: cognitively resilient versus nonresilient, and

emotionally and behaviorally resilient versus nonresilient. Comparisons were made utilizing the Mann-Whitney U-tests (SPSS, Subprogram NPAR tests). If there were significant differences between the mean ranks of the resilient versus nonresilient groups on a specific cluster, Pearson r correlations were then performed on individual variables within the cluster in order to identify which factors were most responsible for explaining the significant difference.

9. Children's drawings, including the stories they told, in addition to emotional indicators on the WPPSI-R were recorded in an effort to assess for presence of emotional trauma.

10. The evaluator's Child Behavior Rating Form was compared with mother's ratings of her child on the CBCL to determine extent of consistency.

11. Internalizing, externalizing, and syndrome scores on the CBCL were calculated in order to describe this sample further.

CHAPTER IV
Results

Before moving to the main results pertaining to the hypotheses, demographic and group characteristics are presented in Tables 5 through 12.

Table 5 presents data related to the families duration of poverty. Total years on AFDC ranged from 1 to 18 years (mean years = 6.35). For this sample, the amount of time from their first episode of homelessness until they moved into their current section 8 housing ranged from .5 to 9 years (mean years = 3.7). The mean average number of moves in the past year was 5 (range 2 to 11), and for the last five years, mean = 14 (range from 3 to 35).

Table 6 shows that over half the mothers in this sample scored in the clinical range on the anxiety and depression measures. Eight women, 47 percent, scored in the clinical range on both. The great majority of these women (65%) have been drug and alcohol free for less than a year. Furthermore, substance abuse has been a problem for all but two of the women in this sample.

Table 7 presents the frequencies of stressful life events which occurred in the mother's life when she was a child. Most of these women came from homes where their parents separated at a young age (82%), 3 of these women (18%) had never met their fathers.

The most striking finding is the amount of family violence these women were exposed to in their childhood years. Ten women (59%) reported that their caretakers had used physical punishment on them like slapping, kicking, and hitting. Eleven
women (65%) reported that family fights occurred on a regular and ongoing basis and, over half (53%), reported having witnessed family violence.

Table 5: Chronicity of Poverty (N=17)

	n	%
Mother's Family of Origin was Supported by Welfare	8	47.2
Total Years Mother has been on AFDC		
1 - 3	3	17.6
3 - 5	5	29.4
5 - 7	3	17.6
7+	6	35.3
Amount of Time from First Episode of Homelessness Until Housed (In Years)		
Within Past Year	2	11.8
1 - 3	4	23.5
3 - 5	3	17.6
5 - 7	6	35.3
7+	2	11.8
Number of Moves Past Year		
0 - 2	4	23.5
3 - 5	6	35.3
6 - 8	5	29.4
9 - 11	2	11.8
Number of Moves Past Five Years		
0 - 4	1	5.9
5 - 9	6	35.3
10 - 14	5	29.4
20 +	5	29.4

Other important findings include that few (3) or 18% had been in foster placements but several (6) or 35% had lived with relatives. There was a strikingly high rate of maternal physical illness (47%) and parental substance abuse. Forty-one percent of the women stated that their mother's and thirty-five percent of their fathers had a drug and/or alcohol problem. In addition, 41% of these mother's fathers spent time in jail when they were growing up.

Another interesting finding was that the majority of these mothers delayed giving birth to their first child until after their 18th birthday, although several became pregnant before that time.

Table 6: Mother's History of Psychological Coping and Current Psychological Status (N=17)

	n	%
History of Psychological Coping		
Mother has made one or more Suicide Attempts	6	35.3
Mother has had a Psychiatric Hospitalization	5	29.4
Mother has been Prescribed Psychiatric Medication	3	17.6
Amount of time Mother has been Clean and Sober		
Drugs & Alcohol not a problem	2	11.8
2+ years	2	11.8
1 - 2 years	2	11.8
Less than 1 year	11	64.7
Current Psychological Status		
Scored in Clinical Range CES-D	10	58.8
Scored in Clinical Range TMAS	9	52.9

Table 8 shows the astonishingly high number of pregnancies among this sample. Fifty-three percent of these women have had 7 or more pregnancies. Equally alarming is the high rate of pregnancy loss. Eight women (47%) had at least one miscarriage, three (18%) gave birth to a child that later died, and two (12%) had a stillbirth. In addition, the majority of these women (65%) have had at least one abortion.

Another striking finding which can be seen in Table 4 is that while nearly half (47%) of these women had a child placed out of their care for a period of over 3 months, only one woman was forced to have her child placed in foster care. The other women were able to find family members who were willing to take their child in. Less than half (41%) of these women have been placed under the supervision of the Department of Social Services.

The majority of these women (65%) have been convicted of a crime. These included: involuntary manslaughter (2); narcotics charges

Table 7: Mother's Childhood Stressful Life Events (N=17)

	n	%
Mother Never Knew One Parent	3	17.6
Mother Sent to Live with Relatives	6	35.3
Mother Placed in Foster Care	3	17.6
Mother's Parents Separated or Divorced	14	82.4
Death of Significant Caregiver or Mother	3	17.6
Death of Sibling	2	11.8
Mother's Mother had Mental Illness	4	23.5
Mother's Father had Mental Illness	1	5.9
Mother had Parent(s) Die as Child	3	17.6
Mother's Mother Abused Alcohol or Drugs	7	41.2
Mother's Father Abused Alcohol or Drugs	6	35.3
Mother's Mother had Physical Illness	8	47.1
Mother's Father had Physical Illness	4	23.5
Mother Physically Abused as Child	10	58.8
Mother Sexually Abused as Child	3	17.6
Mother Witnessed Family Violence	9	52.9
Family Fights in Home	11	64.7
Mother's Mother Spent Time in Jail	2	11.8
Mother's Father Spent Time in Jail	7	41.2
Age Mother Left Home to be on Own		
Under 17 years	7	41.2
17 years +	10	58.8
Mother's Age at First Birth		
Under 18 years	6	35.3
18 years +	11	64.7

(2); shoplifting (2); welfare fraud (2); traffic violations (2); and prostitution (1). The two women charged with involuntary manslaughter murdered their ex-abusers. A total of eight women (47%) have done jail time.

As can be seen in Table 9, these women have been victims of a great deal of violence in their lives. An astronomical 76% have been a victim of a violent crime. These included: being assaulted (6), raped (3), shot (2), stabbed (1), and kidnapped at gunpoint (1). In addition, 88% have been battered by a partner at some time in their lives. Even though these women's lives have stabilized in the past year, 65%

Table 8: Mother's Stressful Life Events as an Adult (N=17)

	n	%
Mother has had one or more Miscarriages	8	47.1
Mother has had one or more Abortions	11	64.7
Mother has had a Stillbirth	2	11.8
Mother gave up a Child for Adoption	1	5.9
Mother gave Birth to a Child that Died	3	17.6
Mother had a Parent Die as an Adult	4	23.5
Mother has had a Close Friend Die as an Adult	5	29.4
Mother has Lost an Important Person in her Life	11	64.7
Mother has Serious Medical Condition	4	23.5
Total number of times Mother has been Pregnant		
Less than 7	8	47.1
7 or more	9	52.9
Mother involved with Child Protective Services	7	41.2
Mother had Child Placed Out of Home	8	47.1
Child Placed in Foster Care	1	5.9
Mother has been Convicted of a Crime	11	64.7
Mother has Spent More than One Week in Jail	8	47.1
Mother ever been on Probation or Parole	8	47.1

reported having been a victim of partner abuse during this time. There was a strong relationship between mothers' having been a victim of domestic violence in the past year and scoring in the clinical range on the CES-D, ($r = .53$; $p < .015$). Just missing significance was the relationship between a high level of anxiety as measured by the TMAS and a history of the mother having been a victim of a violent crime ($r = .40$; $p < .06$).

It is important to note that the rate of childhood sexual abuse is likely to be much higher then reported in this table. Women were not asked directly about childhood sexual abuse, it was only noted if a mother brought it up spontaneously during a interview. The literature is clear that most women do not disclose regarding sexual abuse unless directly asked.

Table 9: Mother's Exposure to Trauma and Victimization (N=17)

	n	%
Mother Victim of a Violent Crime	13	76.4
Mother ever been a Victim of Domestic Violence	15	88.2
Mother Victim of Domestic Violence Past Year	11	64.7
Mother Victim of Childhood Sexual Abuse	3	17.6
Mother Victim of Childhood Physical Abuse	10	58.8

Table 10 shows that the great majority of women in this study (65%) first sought prenatal care during their first trimester. The mean age of the mother at the study child's birth was 24 years (range = 15 to 39). While 53% admitted to using substances during their pregnancy, primarily crack-cocaine and alcohol, only one infant had to stay in the hospital longer than their mother following delivery.

The large number of children (65%) with serious or chronic medical conditions is striking. Most frequent ailments included respiratory ailments such as hay fever (3), bronchitis (2), asthma (2) and respiratory allergies (1). Other common health problems included frequent ear infections (4), and eczema or skin allergies (4).

Table 10: Child's Birth/Health Status (N=17)

	n	%
Month Mother Began Prenatal Care		
1 - 3	11	64.7
4 - 6	3	17.6
6+ or less than 2 Visits	3	17.6
Infant Hospitalized Following Birth	1	5.9
Mother Used Drugs During Pregnancy	9	52.9
Child has a Chronic or Serious Medical Condition	11	64.7
Mother's Age at Child's Birth		
16 years or less	3	17.6
17 years +	14	82.4

Table 11 shows the extent of disruption these children have experienced in their relationship with their mothers, the degree of loss of contact with their fathers, and exposure to trauma and chaos. Interestingly, the rate of separation and divorce among these children's parents (88%) is equal to the rate of divorce and separation of their mother's parents when they were a child (82%). Even more discouraging is the statistic that 71% of these children's mothers hold a negative view of their child's father. The majority of them prefer that the child's father have little contact. The fact that 65% of these children have either a "poor" or "no relationship" with their father bears out this friction. It is not without warrant that these mothers are concerned about their children's contact with their fathers. It was reported that 8 (47%) had spent time in jail and 12 (71%) abused drugs and/or alcohol.

Disruptions in their attachments to their mothers can be seen in the following statistics: 6 (35%) were separated from their mothers for at least 3 months, 15 mothers (88%) disclosed that they had a drug or alcohol problem, 8 (47%) noted a history of mental health problems and 8 (47%) had spent at least one week in jail. Contributing to the risk status of these children is the fact that 53% come from large families with 4 or more children, and in 11 (65%) of these families, there is a sibling with a serious physical or emotional problem.

Perhaps most striking in these children's lives is their exposure to family violence. Thirteen children (76.5%) in this sample had witnessed family violence.

As can be seen in Table 12, the majority of women in this sample (53%) have large support networks consisting of at least six people. Many of the women listed program staff as well as friends and relatives. The majority of this sample also had at least one relative they were close to and whom they saw at least once a month. Since 100% of these women stated that religious faith helped them to get through tough times, it was surprising that only six families (35%) attended church once a month. An unexpected finding was that 47% reported that they had received counseling in the past year. Most of these women had short-term care and were counseled at their church by a trusted clergy member.

Even though the majority of these women have a support network, four reported having "no friends," and an additional woman reported that she had a close friend but did not see her often (less than once a month). Many of the women reported that their old friends were still substance-using and they were afraid to see them for fear that they would get lured back into abusing drugs themselves.

Most women reported attending groups, both through structured programs and independently run 12 step meetings. Five women (29%) in this sample attend a day treatment substance abuse program four days a week.

Table 11: Children's Stressful Life Events (N=17)

	n	%
Child has Witnessed Family Violence	13	76.5
Child has Sibling with a Serious Problem	11	64.7
Number of Children in Family		
1 - 3	8	47.1
4 - 7	9	52.9
Less than Two Years Spacing before Next Child	3	17.6
Child has Never Met Father	3	17.6
Child Separated from Mother for more than 3 Months	6	35.3
Child's Parents are Separated	15	88.2
Child's Parent or Primary Caregiver Died	1	5.9
Child's Mother History of Mental Health Problems	8	47.1
Child's Father History of Mental Health Problems	5	29.4
Child's Mother History of Abusing Alcohol/Drugs	15	88.2
Child's Father History of Abusing Alcohol/Drugs	12	70.6
Child's Mother has Spent Time in Jail	8	47.1
Child's Father has Spent Time in Jail	8	47.1
Child's Mother Involved with Child Protective Services	7	41.2
Child's Mother has Negative View of Child's Father	12	70.6
Mother Clean/Sober Less than One year	11	64.7
Child's Relationship with Father None or "Poor"	11	64.7

The majority of children in this study (53%) have never been enrolled in day care. Five children (29.5%) have attended Head Start, six children (35%) have started school, and two children (12%) were attending a therapeutic nursery school for emotionally troubled preschoolers.

Further highlighting the estranged relationship that these children have with their fathers is the statistic that only five children in this study (29%) saw their father at least once a month.

Table 12: Support Networks: Family's Natural Network, Mother's Agency Involvement, and Child's School or Day Care Enrollment (N=17)

	n	%
Natural Support Network		
Child has Two Caregivers in Home	6	35.3
Child's Father has Ever Paid Child Support	5	29.4
Child Sees Father at Least One Time a Month	5	29.4
Number of Important People in Mother's Life		
1 - 2	1	5.9
3 - 5	5	29.4
6 - 9	9	52.9
10+	2	11.8
Number of Relatives Mother is Close To		
None	2	11.8
1 - 2	7	41.2
3 - 5	4	23.5
6 - 9	3	17.6
10+	1	5.9
Number of Relatives Mother Sees at Least 1x/Month		
None	2	11.8
1 - 2	8	47.1
3 - 5	3	17.6
6 - 9	3	17.6
10+	1	5.9
Number of Close Friends Mother Has		
None	4	23.5
1 - 2	6	35.3
3 - 5	7	41.2
Number of Close Friends Mother Sees at Least Once Per Month		
None	5	29.4
1 - 2	6	35.3
3 - 5	6	35.3
Mother is Currently Working or Volunteering	2	11.8
Family Attends Church at Least Once Per Month	6	35.3
Agency Involvement		
Mother has Received Counseling in Past Year	8	47.1

Table 12 (continued)

	n	%
Mother Attends Drug Treatment Day Program	5	29.4
Number of Groups Mother Attends Per Month		
None	4	23.5
1 - 5	5	29.4
6 - 10	4	23.5
16+	4	23.5
Child's Daycare/School Enrollment		
Amount of Time Child has been in Group Daycare		
None	9	52.9
3 months or less	3	17.6
4 - 12 months	4	23.5
1 year +	1	5.9
Amount of Time Child has been Enrolled at Head Start		
None	12	70.6
Less than 1 year	1	5.9
1 year	2	11.8
1 year +	2	11.8
Amount of Time Child has been Enrolled in Therapeutic Nursery School		
None	15	88.2
At least 6 months	2	11.8
Amount of Time Child has Spent in School		
None	11	64.7
1 year	4	23.5
2 years	2	11.8

Subject Variables

Table 13 shows the results of the children's performance on the WPPSI-R. The mean Full Scale IQ level of the sample was 90.35, SD=13.93, range 73-122. One child scored in the Superior range (5.9%), six children scored in the Average range (35.3%), five children scored in the Low Average range (29.4%), and five children scored in the Borderline range (29.4%). While there was not a significant difference between the children's performance on the Verbal and Performance subtests, they scored somewhat better on the Verbal subtests. As can be seen in Table 13, these children, as a group, performed best on the Picture Completion subtest (mean = 11.24), a test of visual discrimination, and worst on Mazes (mean = 5.24), a test of visual-motor coordination. Nine children (52.9%) showed a good ability to concentrate, persevere even when having difficulty, work carefully and were concerned about their performance. Eight children (47.1%) were easily distracted and frustrated, hyperactive or restless, nervous or high-strung, complained of somatic problems, needed a great deal of encouragement and frequently stated "I don't know," or would not respond at all. Seven parents (41%) reported that their child had a delay in expressive or receptive speech.

Table 13: Children's Cognitive Test Results (N=17)

	Min	Max	Mean	SD
WPPSI-R Full Scale	73	122	90.35	13.93
WPPSI-R Verbal Scale	78	121	92.59	11.26
WPPSI-R Performance Scale	71	124	89.88	16.17
Performance Subtest Scores	**Min**	**Max**	**Mean**	**SD**
Picture Completion	3	18	11.24	4.07
Block Design	3	16	9.12	3.74
Object Assembly	3	14	8.47	3.08
Animal Pegs	1	14	8.47	3.14
Geometric Design	4	15	8.12	3.00
Mazes	1	10	5.24	2.66
Verbal Subtest Scores	**Min**	**Max**	**Mean**	**SD**
Vocabulary	6	13	9.47	1.84
Sentences	5	14	9.29	2.31
Similarities	6	13	9.12	1.87
Arithmetic	5	16	8.94	3.11
Comprehension	5	13	8.18	2.40
Information	3	13	7.88	2.32

Table 14 shows the results of the children's emotional/ behavioral functioning as identified by their mothers. Seven children (41.2%) scored in the clinical range on the Child Behavior Checklist Total Problems scale. Six children (35.3%) fell in the clinical range for a particular syndrome, the majority of these children scoring in the clinical range for more than one syndrome. Most common was Aggressive Behavior (4 children), Delinquent Behavior (3 children), and Destructive Behavior (2 children). One child each scored in the clinical range for Anxious/Depressed, Somatic Problems, Withdrawn, and Thought Problems. Six children (35.3%) exhibited externalizing symptoms, while only one child (5.9%) exhibited internalizing symptoms that were severe enough to fall into the clinical range. Mothers' ratings of their children on the CBCL correlated with the researcher's observational behavioral rating at the .01 level.

The children's drawings were not formally scored because some children had delayed visual-motor skills. The majority of the drawings that were completed lacked body integrity. The absence of arms on the children's drawings was particularly striking. There was a wide range of affects expressed in the stories the children told about their drawings, with some children refusing to say anything about their drawing.

Six children (35.3%) had emotional indicators on the WPPSI-R test. These included responses to questions such as, (Q)"What is a knife?" (R) "I cut my leg with it," "To cut my hand," "Sharp, stick it right here (pointed to neck)," "Could cut people or could cut chicken," "Cut stuff . . . cut your body, cut your neck off, cut meat with it." Another question was, "How is a knife and a piece of broken glass alike?" Response, "And the blood came out of their face, and a piece of hand came off when they cut their belly." Question, "How are happy and sad alike?" Response, "I get mad and happy and sad. Make your face change and make your brain want to jump out the window." Question, "Boys grow up to be men, and girls grow up to be _____?" Response, "Nothing." Question, "What is a swing?" Response, "You push higher, and the birds will hit you and hurt you." Several children talked about their losses as they looked at different pictures. Common responses were, "I had a doggie, but somebody stole it," or, "I had a fish, but he died." One girl, when asked what you should do if a friend is crying, responded, "I don't have no friends."

When the mothers were asked to discuss the best things about their children, most listed characteristics such as being smart, loving, aggressive, assertive, and independent. Particularly valued were children who loved, watched out for, and took care of their younger siblings. Children were also highly regarded for assisting in the care of their mothers' babies (fixing bottles and changing diapers), and looking out for and taking care of their mothers. One mother referred positively to her daughter as "a mother little girl." Another mother reported, "My son says he has two babies, me and his little brother."

When asked to discuss what concerned them most about their children, mothers reported most frequently their concern with their children's speech. They stated that their children were not talking or could not be understood, and that their children were not able to understand what was said to them. Other responses included, "going to school in drug-infested area," "not friendly towards others" or "she doesn't like people," "whining," "wetting herself during the day," "cries very easily," "too sensitive for no reason," and "too scared and won't hit back." Many mothers mentioned temper tantrums and feigned illnesses and adult behavior such as, "She's a little too grown for her age."

Table 14: Children's Emotional/Behavioral Test Results (N=17)

	Min	Max	Mean	SD
CBCL Total Problem Score	47	70	55.71	10.02
CBCL Internalizing Score	43	70	53.00	7.72
CBCL Externalizing Score	38	74	57.24	11.29

Table 15 shows that the majority of mothers self-reported symptoms indicative of both depression and anxiety. Ten mothers (58.8%) scored in the clinical range on The Center for Epidemiologic Studies Depression Scale while nine mothers (52.9%) scored in the clinical range on the Taylor Manifest Anxiety Scale.

Table 15: Mother's Psychological Test Results (N=17)

	Min	Max	Mean	SD
CES-Depression Scale	4	34	17.65	7.80
Taylor Manifest Anxiety Scale	8	46	21.71	10.24

Study Hypotheses

Hypothesis #1: Mothers' resilient status, as measured by her current level of psychological distress, obtained level of academic and occupational competency, and past history of psychological coping, will be associated with her child's emotional/behavioral resiliency.

This hypothesis was tested by comparing the mothers of children who were in the normal range on the CBCL with the mothers of children who fell into the clinical range. The Mann-Whitney U-tests (SPSS, Subprogram NPAR tests) were compared on the mean ranks for the two groups. Table 16 shows, as predicted, that resilient childrens' mothers current psychological functioning was significantly better than the nonresilient children (z = 2.28; $p<.03$). The most significant contributing factor was mother's score on the Taylor Manifest Anxiety Scale (Pearson r = .51; $p<.02$). Mother's score on the CES-D was not significant (Pearson r = .32; $p<.10$).

As can be seen in Table 16, group differences on Mother's Competence just missed significance (z = 1.81; $p<.07$). In order of importance, was mother's previous salary (Pearson r = .62; $p<.004$), occupation (Pearson r = .49; $p<.022$), and educational attainment (Pearson r = .40; $p<.05$).

Mother's history of past psychological coping bore no relationship to child's current resilient emotional/behavioral status.

Hypothesis #2: Mother's stressful life events, particularly those that limit her availability to her child (e.g. drug use, separations, domestic violence) will be related to child's emotional/behavioral competency.

Table 17 shows that mother's childhood and adult stressful life events did not significantly relate to children's resilient status except in the area of mother's victimization. When the Mann Whitney U-test was used to compare the mean ranks for the two groups, it was found that resilient children's mothers scored significantly lower (z = 2.06; $p<.043$) on the items contributing to the trauma and victimization cluster. As can be seen in Table 17, two factors in the cluster were significant. These included: mother having been a victim of domestic violence in the past year (Pearson r = .55; $p<.01$); and mother having been a victim of a violent crime (Pearson r = .52, $p<.016$).

Hypothesis #3: The degree of economic hardship a family has endured will be associated with children's emotional/behavioral and cognitive competency.

The variables included in the chronicity of poverty cluster (amount of time homeless, number of moves made in the past five years, and length of time family has been on welfare) were not significantly associated with either children's emotional/behavioral competency (z = 1.4; $p <.16$) or their cognitive resilience (z= 1.3; $p <.19$).

Hypothesis # 4: It is predicted that the more resources that the mother has available to her and her child in the way of natural support systems and agency support the better off the child will fare in terms of emotional/behavioral functioning and intellectual competence.

Table 16: Comparisons Among Child's Emotional/Behavioral Competence and Mother's Current Psychological Status, Competency, and History of Psychological Coping (N=17)

	Resilient Children		Nonresilient Children				
Mother's Psychological Coping	*M* Rank	n	*M* Rank	n	Z		p
	6.85	10	12.07	7	2.28		.03*
						r	p
TMAS						.51	.019*
CES-D						.32	.10
Mother's Competency	*M* Rank	n	*M* Rank	n	Z		p
	10.85	10	6.36	7	1.81		.07
						r	p
Education						.40	.05*
Longest Job						.04	.44
Salary						.62	.004**
Occupation						.49	.022*
Mother's History of Psychological Coping	*M* Rank	n	*M* Rank	n	Z		p
	9.50	10	8.29	7	.49		.67

* = $p < .05$
** = $p < .01$

Table 17: Comparisons Between Mother's Stressful Life Events and Child's Emotional/Behavioral Functioning (N=17)

	Resilient Children			Nonresilient Children		
	M Rank	n	M Rank	n	Z	p
Mother's Stressful Life Events as Child/Adolescent	7.80	10	10.71	7	1.18	.27
Mother's Stressful Life Events as Adult	8.65	10	9.50	7	.35	.74
Mother's Victimization	6.95	10	11.93	7	2.06	.04*
		r			p	
Victim of a Violent Crime		.53			.016*	
Victim of Domestic Violence past year		.55			.01**	
Ever a Victim of Domestic Violence		.065			.40	
Mother Victim of Childhood Sexual Abuse		.24			.18	
Mother Victim of Childhood Physical Abuse		.03			.46	

* = p<.05
** = p<.01

Table 18 clearly indicates that natural support systems were not related, as hypothesized, to either children's cognitive or emotional/behavioral resiliency. In fact, nonresilient children came from families with larger natural support networks. Agency support was however related, as predicted, to emotional/behavioral resiliency (z = 2.31; *p*<.025) but not to cognitive status. The only significant contributing factor was the number of groups mother attends per month (r = .49; *p*<.023). As Table 18 shows, the differences between the two groups was not in the area of participation in church groups or attendance at drug treatment programs. Alternatively, the resilient children's mothers attended more self-help groups (NA, AA, CA) and received more agency support in the areas of parenting and non-drug treatment groups.

Table 18 also shows that amount of schooling was significantly related to cognitive competency (z = 3.11; *p*<.001) but not to emotional/behavioral functioning. Accounting for the largest amount of variance was participation in Head Start (r = .60; *p*<.005), followed by enrollment in school (r = .46; *p*<.030). Attendance in day care or a therapeutic nursery school were both negatively correlated with cognitive competency.

Hypothesis # 5: Children's cognitive and emotional/behavioral functioning will be effected by their birth and health status, stressful life events, the number of children in the family, and the child's ordinal position.

This hypothesis was supported only for children's cognitive competency being related to their birth and health status (z = 2.5; *p*<.014). Table 19 shows that accounting for this significance were two factors: time at which mother began her prenatal care (Pearson r = .42; *p*<.047); and whether she used drugs during her pregnancy (Pearson r = .41; *p*<.052). Child's ordinal position, older children faring better, just missed significance (Pearson r = .39; *p*<.058).

Another significant unpredicted finding was that older mothers at the birth of their first child, had preschoolers who were more cognitively competent (Pearson r = .59; *p*<.006).

Table 18: Comparisons among Social Support, Agency Support, Schooling and Children's Emotional/Behavioral and Cognitive Competency (N=17)

Mother's Natural Support System

	Resilient Children		Nonresilient Children			
	M Rank	n	M Rank	n	Z	p
Cognitive	8.00	7	9.70	10	.69	.54
Emotional/Behavioral	8.65	10	9.50	7	.34	.74

Agency Support

	Resilient Children		Nonresilient Children			
	M Rank	n	M Rank	n	Z	p
Cognitive	10.00	7	8.30	10	.70	.54
Emotional/Behavioral	11.30	10	5.71	7	2.3	.025*

	r	p
Number of Groups Mother Attends /month	.49	.023*
Mother in Counseling past year	.31	.11
Mother Attends Drug Treatment Day Program	.015	.48

Table 18 (continued)

Schooling

	Resilient Children		Nonresilient Children			
	M Rank	n	*M* Rank	n	Z	p
Emotional/Behavioral	10.70	10	6.57	7	1.7	.11
Cognitive	13.36	7	5.95	10	3.1	.001***

	r	p
Head Start	.60	.005*
School	.46	.030*
Day care	-.09	.36
Therapeutic Daycare	-.305	.12

* = *p* < .05
*** = *p* <.001

Table 19: Relationship Among Children's Birth and Health Status, Stressful Life Events, Family Size, Ordinal Position and Their Emotional/Behavioral and Cognitive Competency (N=17)

Child's Birth/Health Status

	Resilient Children		Nonresilient Children			
	M Rank	n	M Rank	n	Z	p
Emotional/Behavioral	8.55	10	9.64	7	.45	.67
Cognitive	5.43	7	11.50	10	2.5	.014*

	r	p
Mother's Prenatal Care	.42	.047*
Drug Use During Pregnancy	.41	.05*
Mother's Age at Child's Birth	.39	.06
Child has Chronic Medical Condition	.38	.065

Table 19: (continued)

Child's Stressful Life Events

	Resilient Children		Nonresilient Children			
	M Rank	n	M Rank	n	Z	p
Emotional/Behavioral	9.75	10	7.93	7	.74	.47
Cognitive	6.50	7	10.75	10	1.7	.09
Family Size						
			r		p	
Emotional/Behavioral			.17		.26	
Cognitive			.17		.29	
Ordinal Position						
			r		p	
Emotional/Behavioral			.00		.50	
Cognitive			.39		.058	

SUMMARY OF RESULTS

1. Mother's current psychological functioning, as measured by the TMAS and CES-D, was significantly related to children's emotional/behavioral functioning. In addition, the mother's exposure to trauma and victimization, particularly if she had been the victim of a violent crime or battered by a partner during the previous year, was significant. The amount of agency support the mother received in the form of groups was also significantly related to children's emotional/behavioral competency.

2. Most predictive of children's cognitive competency were mother's age at the time of her first birth, whether the child had attended Head Start or regular school, and the child's birth and health status. Mothers who started prenatal care earlier and those who did not use drugs during their pregnancies delivered children who were more cognitively competent.

3. Just missing statistical significance was mother's competency status. Her educational level, previous salary, and occupation appeared to be potentially important factors.

4. Mother's and children's stressful life events, the family's chronicity of poverty and amount of social support, and family size all appeared unrelated to cognitive competency. There was a nonsignificant trend toward oldest children performing better on cognitive tasks, compared to their own age group, than younger children.

5. None of the mother's other childhood or adult stressful life events were related to children's emotional/behavioral competency. Chronicity of poverty and the family's natural support networks were also unrelated.

6. The mean overall Full Scale IQ level of the sample was in the Average range. The children as a whole performed best on a subtest that measured visual discrimination and worst on a subtest that measured visual-motor coordination.

7. Children's drawings could not be rated for emotional indicators because of the children's undeveloped visual-motor skills. Many children presented with emotional indicators on the WPPSI-R test and told stories about the pictures they drew that were indicative of underlying emotional trauma.

8. Forty-one percent of the children scored in the clinical range on the CBCL. All of these children, with the exception of one, had problems of an externalizing nature.

9. Sixty-five percent of the mothers scored in the clinical range on either the CES-D or TMAS, indicating a high level of depression and anxiety. Forty-seven percent of the mothers scored in the clinical range on both scales.

CHAPTER V

Discussion

This study investigated the developmental status of young African-American children who have experienced an episode of homelessness. The main objective was to identify the characteristics and life circumstances of resilient children. This was done by examining the relationship between a number of personal and ecological factors of a psychological and social nature. The need for this study was based on the soaring rates of homelessness among families containing young children.

It is important to note that this was not a homogeneous sample. The children's mothers' pathways into and out of homelessness varied tremendously, as did the length of time they were homeless, the number of moves they made in the past five years, their dependence on welfare, and their family backgrounds.

Some commonalities did exist, however. Most of the women had completed high school or its equivalency, were eighteen years old or older at the birth of their first child, and had large support networks made up of family, friends, and agency staff. While the majority of these mothers sought early prenatal care for the study children, nearly the same number admitted to abusing drugs during their pregnancies. In addition to long-standing substance abuse, these mothers had multiple pregnancies and pregnancy losses. An important finding was that a large number of these women had experienced severed or disrupted relationships and a high rate of trauma and victimization starting at a young age and continuing through to their present-day lives.

The following commonalities existed among the children. The majority came from large families having four or more siblings, but were spaced more than two years apart. Of importance was the fact that most had a sibling who had a serious emotional problem or physical condition. These children's mothers and fathers had significant drug histories and contact with the criminal justice system, a large number having spent time in jail. In addition, most of these children's parents had separated, and typically their mothers held a negative view of their fathers. The children, for the most part, had poor relationships with their fathers and very little contact with them. Only five children (29%) saw their fathers at least once a month.

What was so impressive was the extent to which these families persevered against all odds. Despite life situations that held them down—violence, poverty, neighborhood gangs, dehumanizing institutions, racism, loss of friends and family, and overall bad luck—they found the strength to get into drug treatment, which was the first step in stabilizing their lives. Despite limited resources and dangerous neighborhoods, they continue to set goals and work toward bettering their lives and those of their children.

It is impossible to capture on any stressful life events inventory the magnitude of danger ever-present in these families' lives. Gunshots heard in the distance or as close as the front yard during the interviews were reminders of the war zone in which many of these families live. The stresses in not being able to allow one's children out of the house to play, or fears of what will happen to them as they walk to or home from school, take their toll.

While six children, three boys and three girls, scored in the competent range on both the cognitive and emotional/behavioral instruments, only one child, a 6-year-old girl, could be defined as resilient on all the measures. The other children had emotional indicators either on the WPPSI-R or on their projective drawing, which suggested underlying psychological trauma. It is noteworthy that the one resilient child has had the longest school attendance and obtained the highest Full Scale IQ.

As a group, the mean of this sample's IQ scores fell into the Average range. This is an encouraging finding, which indicates that many of these children have the strengths to succeed in school. The IQ test is one of the best predictors of school performance (Zigler & Trickett, 1978). An even distribution, 43% of the boys and 40% of the girls, scored in the competent/resilient range.

Contrary to other studies (Murphy & Moriarty, 1976; Rutter, 1970; Werner & Smith, 1982), boys in this study fared better than girls. In the emotional/behavioral domain, 86% of the boys received ratings from their mothers that placed them in the resilient range, whereas only 40% of the girls did. This may be due to some of the following factors: (1) mothers may be more connected to, and aware of, their daughters' feelings and actions; (2) due to daughters' need to identify with their mothers, they may be more susceptible to their mothers' psychological state; and (3) girls may be more psychologically vulnerable to witnessing their mothers being battered.

With the exception of three children, evidence of emotional trauma was seen in all of this sample, with 14 of the 17 children presenting with depressive, violent, and self-destructive imagery. Many of the children's drawings could not be scored, due to the children's lack of exposure to and experience with drawing and their visual-motor delays. Several of the children who were able to complete the task drew figures that were cause for concern. Some of the drawings consisted of disorganized body parts, reflecting a lack of sense of self and body integrity. Other figures had a striking absence of body parts, particularly arms. These images may reflect the children's inner convictions that they cannot reach out too much because of a need to defend themselves from an environment that they have experienced as hostile, unpredictable, and threatening.

Children's stories about their pictures ranged from a manifestation of positive mood ("It's about me going to school, and I'm playing a computer game—I'm happy") to benign activity ("A person riding a bicycle") to themes of loss ("This is a mother and a child—black peoples—she wants her mamma and daddy—she wants her daddy") and anger ("This must be my dad standing trying to get cereal. He's a little too mad"). The children were not without hope in regards to their current situations. One child, for example, stated, "This is Superman. He gets there in the morning. He's going to help."

One common theme related to children's missing their absent fathers. Another common theme that emerged in this study was an attempt by the children to be protective of their mothers and also to express a great deal of concern for them. They oftentimes strived to meet their mothers' needs when their own needs were not getting met. These children had an empathic ability both to sense their mothers' tension and to comfort their mothers when stressed. One mother proudly described her son as "the man of the house," and another mother boasted of her daughter, "She's a mother little girl." The mothers in this study frequently reported that they highly valued their children for taking care of them. In sum, the findings from this study suggest that these children's environmental experiences have not left them unscathed, particularly in the emotional and behavioral domains.

FINDINGS RELATED TO CHILDREN'S EMOTIONAL/BEHAVIORAL FUNCTIONING

As hypothesized, mothers' levels of psychological distress were positively related to their children's emotional/behavioral functioning. There was a strong relationship between a mother's depressed and anxious state and her child's emotional and behavioral adjustment. Mothers who were able to model a resilient stance had children who were able to do so as well. This researcher believes that the high rate of clinical depression and anxiety in this sample of women is related to their recent withdrawal from drugs and alcohol, history of victimization, and their many life stressors.

The majority of women in this sample have been clean and sober for less than a year. While they previously turned to drugs to self-medicate their pain, they are now in the process of developing new, more effective coping strategies that have not yet crystallized. The present researcher's impression from speaking with these women was that many were really struggling to remain clean and sober. In fact, several had relapsed. When people with very limited resources are struggling with symptoms associated with clinical depression and high anxiety in addition to multiple daily stressors, it is difficult to be sensitive and attuned to anyone else's needs, particularly young children who demand so much attention.

While mothers' early life experiences bore no direct relationship with children's emotional/behavioral resiliency, one has to wonder about the impact that these experiences have had on the mothers' life course and current psychological status. Not only do these women have models of disrupted relationships, starting from when they were very young, but they also have many other unresolved traumas that they carry forward with them from those early years. These traumatic experiences not only serve to challenge and undermine the mothers' ability to parent, but they also were likely contributors to their history of substance abuse and current highly anxious and depressed state.

An encouraging finding uncovered by this study was that mothers' involvement with social service agencies was significantly related to their children's superior emotional/behavioral functioning. It was striking how many women included agency staff in their support networks. Agency involvement has likely helped these mothers not to be pushed beyond their tolerance level. It is also likely that the support they have received from staff members and peers was passed on to their children. The supportive relationships likely aided in the development of the mothers' self-esteem. This, in turn, impacted not only on the confidence they felt in their parenting role but also on their availability and stability. Having groups and individuals the mothers could count on in their own lives likely helped them to be more consistent and available to their children, increasing the likelihood for secure, trusting, relationships to evolve. Actual parenting information received from program participation also may have improved the mothers' understanding of their children's developmental needs, increasing the possibility that they would respond to their children in more appropriate and empathic ways.

An interesting and unexpected finding was that a family's natural support network bore no relationship to the child's resiliency. An understanding of this finding came from the women themselves. Many of the women described relatives who burdened them with requests for housing, money, and items they could not afford to give. There was little reciprocity described in the contacts these women had, particularly with family, but also with friends and relatives.

Inconsistent with past studies, the researcher did not find that the mothers' status on the depression scale contributed to their increased tendency to report maladaptive behavioral manifestations in their children. It has been proposed previously that parents' ratings can be affected by their own adjustment (Sandler & Block, 1979) and that mothers' depression leads to lowered tolerance of behaviors and their increased tendency to rate their children negatively (Hammen, 1991). In fact, in the present study, there was a very significant correlation between mothers' responses on the CBCL and the researcher's behavioral ratings of the children.

An additional finding in this study was that mothers' psychological status, as indicated by the extent of their depression and anxiety, was more important than any life events. The only significant life events were related to the mothers' exposure to trauma and victimization. There was a strong relationship between mothers' current high level of depression and their having been victims of domestic violence in the preceding year. Just missing significance was the relationship between mothers' high anxiety level and having been a victim of a violent crime.

The findings in this study validate those of other studies which state that children suffer extreme emotional trauma by witnessing their mothers' being battered. This study is another confirmation that children cannot tolerate witnessing loved ones' being abused. Young children are devastated because they are powerless to stop the violence, which leaves them feeling helpless, terrified, and insecure. At a time when children need to feel safe and secure in order to form strong interpersonal attachments and develop a sense of confidence in their environment, the chaos of abuse interferes and results in an environment where there is typically unsteady nurturance and support. Children have a loss of faith that others will be able to protect them and that they will be able to find a safe place to which they can retreat.

These children are continually aroused by their environment but have no way to relieve their stress. It is an environment which teaches them that assault is an acceptable way to handle conflict. The children in this study have not learned appropriate controls, as is shown by the high frequency of externalizing behaviors that they exhibit. There is also the danger that children will imitate or model their behavior after the abuser, a response commonly termed "identifying with the aggressor," which can lead to an intergenerational continuation of familial violence.

Inconsistent with previous studies, this study revealed that girls rather than boys showed a high rate of externalizing behavior. Five out of six girls (83%), whose aggressive and destructive behaviors were severe enough that they fell into the clinical range, had mothers who had been battered during the preceding year. These girls were probably not only imitating behaviors observed in their home, but also attempting to release a high anxiety level that was stirred up by exposure to such chaos and violence.

The boys may have inhibited their aggression, knowing that their fathers were viewed so negatively and had been, in many instances, thrown out of the house. They may have feared that the rage that their mothers felt toward their fathers might be acted out on them or, more importantly, that they might lose their mothers' love if they acted aggressively.

It is important to note that the mothers in this study often fought back in their own self-defense. In the preceding year, 7 of the 11 (64%) women who had been battered reported having struck back. Two (12%) of the women in this sample have histories of inflicting serious enough wounds on their partners that they had to be hospitalized, while two other women's retaliations resulted in their partners' deaths. Therefore, the girls in this study have been exposed to mothers who were not passive victims but who took action. These girls may have modeled their behavior after their mothers' own retaliatory and aggressive acts.

The girls' externalizing behaviors may have been the result of several factors: (1) the children may have identified with a highly anxious mother and, not having neither the capacity to tolerate the strong emotions or the means to diffuse them, acted them out; (2) the children may have reenacted behaviors by which they themselves have been traumatized, in an attempt to work through them and get some control over their environment; (3) the children may simply have been imitating behavior that they have witnessed at another time; (4) the children may have acted out in an attempt to capture their mothers' attention; or (5) the children may have been attempting to rouse their mothers out of a depression or to be noticed in an environment where it is hard to be seen.

It has been reported that externalizing behaviors undermine school adjustment and cause damage to social integration (Jaffe, Wolfe, & Wilson, 1990). Children who act out lack inner controls or higher levels of defensive techniques. A vicious cycle is created in which trauma stunts intellectual development, without which there are few alternatives for coping. Children who have the cognitive ability to more fully understand the situation under which the abuse occurs are better able to master stress and maintain self-control. Anthony (1987) termed this ability "representational competence." Children lacking this capacity frequently attribute the violence in their homes to something they have caused, resulting in a very negative sense of self.

Children who feel that things happen independently of their actions tend to give up, feel hopeless, and not persevere. This orientation, frequently referred to as "learned helplessness," has grave consequences for children's intellectual development. In the present study, 7 of 11 children (64%) whose mothers had recently been battered, scored below average on the IQ test. Finding evidence of learned helplessness in young children, Seligman (1975) concluded, "What is often passed off as retardation or an IQ deficit may be the result of learned helplessness. . . . Intelligence, no matter how high, cannot manifest itself if the child believes that his own actions have no effect" (p. 154).

There is evidence that just like the mothers in this study who presented with post-traumatic responses to their abuse and victimization, the children, too, presented with symptoms of having been traumatized. Increased arousal was one such symptom. It is particularly noteworthy that this sample scored highest on the Picture Completion subtest on the WPPSI-R, a subtest that captures children's hypervigilance in regards to social situations. These children have learned, at a young age, to be on guard as an adaptive survival and coping strategy. They have become proficient at scanning their environment for social clues, having learned the necessity for living defensively both within their homes and in their neighborhoods.

FINDINGS RELATED TO CHILDREN'S COGNITIVE FUNCTIONING

The findings in this study corroborate research by Molnar et al. (1991) of the Banks Street College, who found that children with as little as three months' exposure to Head Start performed more age-appropriately on cognitive tasks. For this sample of children, Head Start was the most important contributor to competent cognitive functioning. School attendance also was correlated with these children's cognitive performance.

While the children, as a group, performed in a superior manner on the Picture Completion subtest, which required skills they had developed, they did not do as well on other subtests that did not directly relate to their environmental experiences. Of interest was the fact that day care was negatively correlated with intelligence as measured by an IQ test. One wonders about the quality, freedom from chaos, and consistency of the day care these children received.

Another significant finding was that children whose mothers received early prenatal care and who did not use drugs during their pregnancies had children who later performed significantly better on the cognitive test. This finding underscores the importance of constitutional factors in an environment so heavily laden with other risk factors. Having the benefits of a sound constitution helped these children negotiate the many other barriers.

Eldest children were also at an advantage, which is consistent with the findings of other researchers (Werner & Smith, 1982). Having a parent to oneself without having to share her (or him) with other siblings for a period of time aided in their resilience. Similarly, children whose mothers were older at the time of their first child's birth received higher scores. It is assumed that these mothers were able to benefit from more education and longer work histories before having children, adding to their own competency, which was then passed on to their children.

CONCLUSION

The results of this study emphasize the importance of the ecological model (Bronfenbrenner, 1986) and the transactional perspective (Sameroff & Chandler, 1975). These approaches acknowledge the impact on the functioning of families of various factors, such as external environments, intrafamilial processes, genetic influences, and individual characteristics. Significant factors in the present study included variables representing all of these areas. They included: the children's constitutional status and ordinal position; the mothers' psychological functioning and history of being a victim of a violent crime; the presence of extrafamilial support for both child and mother; the occurrence of violence in the home directed against the mother; and the age at which the mother gave birth to her first child.

While these children performed satisfactorily on cognitive tasks, the results of the psychological testing indicate alarming emotional difficulties. It is evident that these children's life experiences have already impacted on their sense of safety and security in their world. They can be seen as secondary victims of their mothers' substance abuse and of the violence that their mothers have endured. Alternatively, they can be seen as secondary benefactors of their mothers' occupational competence and involvement with social service agencies.

Children's expectations about the world are built on ideas they have about relationships that occur early in life. These early relational models tend to persist and impact on their future. It is of the utmost importance that these children acquire a sense of worthiness and a view of the world as relatively safe so that they will not take on an attitude of futility. Giving these mothers social service support is one way of aiding their children's development. If a sense of hopefulness can be instilled in these children there is a greater chance that they will succeed in school and in the world in general. Otherwise, they are at risk for repeating a cycle of despair from which their mothers are currently struggling to escape.

LIMITATIONS OF THIS STUDY

It is unclear how representative this sample is of mothers who have had a history of homelessness. The women in this study had a strikingly high level of educational attainment and extensive support networks, and the majority sought prenatal care in their first trimester. Therefore, the results may not be readily transferable to other mothers and children who have experienced homelessness.

A significant limitation of the study is that these children were only assessed at one point in time in regard to competence. It is unknown what far-reaching effects a homeless experience, with all the associated stressors, might have on a child's adaption at a later stage of development. Another limitation is that the children were not assessed prior to their experience of homelessness, to isolate out precisely how that experience may have impacted on their developmental status. There was also no control group of low-income children, which could have served to differentiate factors that related specifically to homelessness and those that are correlated with poverty status.

Other limitations relate to the children's lack of motivation due to their having no prior experience in achievement situations. Many of the children had not been in school or day-care environments that require sustained attention, provide an opportunity to problem-solve, and expose them to information that would have allowed them to receive a higher score on the WPPSI-R. Children of color, particularly from low-income backgrounds, consistently score lower on cognitive tests. This relates to the standardization sample on which the test was normed and the context in which a child develops. What may be an adaptive skill in one environment may not be in another. The survival skills of this sample of children may not have been tapped. In sum, all these factors point to the fact that the scores on the WPPSI-R that these children received are not likely to be a true indicator of their actual abilities.

Another limitation relates to using the mothers as the only informants about their children's behavior. Ideally, other respondents who see the children in other settings should be asked to record their observations, too. However, since these children have made so many residential moves, few of them have had any recent or stable day-care or school experiences, so finding such additional reliable observers would be difficult, if not impossible.

CLINICAL IMPLICATIONS OF THIS STUDY

While obtaining a home is an important first intervention for these families, it is not enough. Clearly, these families' lives are not yet stable. Improving environmental circumstances has everything to do with lessening children's exposure to risk factors and increasing the number of protective factors on which they can draw. Children need to feel secure, to receive consistent, empathic caregiving in order to develop a positive self-concept and realize their cognitive capabilities. They need to be involved in therapeutic Head Start or other quality day-care programs, organizations like the YMCA or YWCA, Boys and Girls Clubs, and Big Brother and Big Sister programs in which they will have the opportunity to engage in activities that promote self-esteem, mastery, and the formation of supportive relationships with caring and trustworthy adults.

Likewise, mothers need to be involved in activities that help them master their own feelings of helplessness by giving them skills and resources. The mothers in this study have a great deal of potential, as is reflected in their academic achievements. They need experiences that will allow them to feel successful and valued and to obtain a sense of accomplishment. At the same time, these mothers have experienced a great deal of trauma and need assistance recovering and developing coping strategies to deal with their stressful environments. Psychological intervention would aim at decreasing mothers' high anxiety levels and feelings of depression, freeing them up to be more psychologically available to their children. In addition, counseling that assists in helping mothers better understand their children's feelings will help them to respond more empathically.

Involvement in groups of women with whom they can share a sense of communality will not only give these mothers a sense of belonging but will also help them to reestablish trust that they have lost both in themselves and in their relationships with others. Until their basic needs for security, affiliation, and trust are met, they will not be able to take adequate psychological care of their children.

One of the most important findings of this study was that emotionally resilient mothers had better-adjusted children. Therefore, mothers need to be buffered from their extremely stressful life circumstances by having access to a wide range of services so that they do not become overwhelmed and they will be better able to be supportive of and nurturant to their children. Some of these services may include high-quality child care and emergency respite, parent education, transportation to meetings, and availability of emergency food, clothing, and other necessities. In addition, the mothers need access to counseling for substance abuse, domestic violence and psychological issues. Church leaders to offer spiritual support as well as mentors to offer friendship, educational and vocational guidance will assist women in feeling hopeful about their futures. Job training, continuing education, and occupational placement are other necessary services that will promote positive outcomes.

Child Behavior Checklist/4-18

CHILD BEHAVIOR CHECKLIST FOR AGES 4–18

For office use only
ID #

Please Print

CHILD'S FULL NAME: FIRST · MIDDLE · LAST

PARENTS' USUAL TYPE OF WORK, even if not working now. (Please be specific—for example, auto mechanic, high school teacher, homemaker, laborer, lathe operator, shoe salesman, army sergeant.)

SEX ☐ Boy ☐ Girl
AGE
ETHNIC GROUP OR RACE

FATHER'S TYPE OF WORK: _____

TODAY'S DATE
Mo. _____ Date _____ Yr. _____

CHILD'S BIRTHDATE
Mo. _____ Date _____ Yr. _____

MOTHER'S TYPE OF WORK: _____

THIS FORM FILLED OUT BY:

GRADE IN SCHOOL _____

Please fill out this form to reflect *your* view of the child's behavior even if other people might not agree. Feel free to print additional comments beside each item and in the spaces provided on page 2.

NOT ATTENDING SCHOOL ☐

☐ Mother (full name) _____
☐ Father (full name) _____
☐ Other—name & relationship to child: _____

I. Please list the sports your child most likes to take part in. For example: swimming, baseball, skating, skate boarding, bike riding, fishing, etc.

☐ None

	Compared to others of the same age, about how much time does he/she spend in each?				Compared to others of the same age, how well does he/she do each one?			
	Don't Know	Less Than Average	Average	More Than Average	Don't Know	Below Average	Average	Above Average
a. _____	☐	☐	☐	☐	☐	☐	☐	☐
b. _____	☐	☐	☐	☐	☐	☐	☐	☐
c. _____	☐	☐	☐	☐	☐	☐	☐	☐

II. Please list your child's favorite hobbies, activities, and games, other than sports. For example: stamps, dolls, books, piano, crafts, cars, singing, etc. (Do *not* include listening to radio or TV.)

☐ None

	Compared to others of the same age, about how much time does he/she spend in each?				Compared to others of the same age, how well does he/she do each one?			
	Don't Know	Less Than Average	Average	More Than Average	Don't Know	Below Average	Average	Above Average
a. _____	☐	☐	☐	☐	☐	☐	☐	☐
b. _____	☐	☐	☐	☐	☐	☐	☐	☐
c. _____	☐	☐	☐	☐	☐	☐	☐	☐

III. Please list any organizations, clubs, teams, or groups your child belongs to.

☐ None

	Compared to others of the same age, how active is he/she in each?			
	Don't Know	Less Active	Average	More Active
a. _____	☐	☐	☐	☐
b. _____	☐	☐	☐	☐
c. _____	☐	☐	☐	☐

IV. Please list any jobs or chores your child has. For example: paper route, babysitting, making bed, working in store, etc. (Include *both* paid and unpaid jobs and chores.)

☐ None

	Compared to others of the same age, how well does he/she carry them out?			
	Don't Know	Below Average	Average	Above Average
a. _____	☐	☐	☐	☐
b. _____	☐	☐	☐	☐
c. _____	☐	☐	☐	☐

Please Print

V. 1. About how many close friends does your child have? ☐ None ☐ 1 ☐ 2 or 3 ☐ 4 or more
(Do *not* include brothers & sisters)

2. About how many times a week does your child do things with any friends outside of regular school hours?
(Do *not* include brothers & sisters) ☐ Less than 1 ☐ 1 or 2 ☐ 3 or more

VI. Compared to others of his/her age, how well does your child:

		Worse	About Average	Better	
a.	Get along with his/her brothers & sisters?	☐	☐	☐	☐ Has no brothers or sisters
b.	Get along with other kids?	☐	☐	☐	
c.	Behave with his/her parents?	☐	☐	☐	
d.	Play and work alone?	☐	☐	☐	

VII. 1. For ages 6 and older—performance in academic subjects. ☐ Does not attend school because _____

Check a box for each subject that child takes	Failing	Below Average	Average	Above Average
a. Reading, English, or Language Arts	☐	☐	☐	☐
b. History or Social Studies	☐	☐	☐	☐
c. Arithmetic or Math	☐	☐	☐	☐
d. Science	☐	☐	☐	☐

Other academic subjects—for example: computer courses, foreign language, business. Do *not* include gym, shop, driver's ed., etc.

	Failing	Below Average	Average	Above Average
e. _____	☐	☐	☐	☐
f. _____	☐	☐	☐	☐
g. _____	☐	☐	☐	☐

2. Does your child receive special remedial services
or attend a special class or special school? ☐ No ☐ Yes—kind of services, class, or school:

3. Has your child repeated any grades? ☐ No ☐ Yes—grades and reasons:

4. Has your child had any academic or other problems in school? ☐ No ☐ Yes—please describe:

When did these problems start?

Have these problems ended? ☐ No ☐ Yes—when?

Does your child have any illness or disability (either physical or mental)? ☐ No ☐ Yes—please describe:

What concerns you most about your child?

Please describe the best things about your child:

Below is a list of items that describe children and youth. For each item that describes your child *now or within the past 6 months*, please circle the *2* if the item is *very true or often true* of your child. Circle the *1* if the item is *somewhat or sometimes true* of your child. If the item is *not true* of your child, circle the *0*. Please answer all items as well as you can, even if some do not seem to apply to your child.

Please Print

0 = Not True (as far as you know)   1 = Somewhat or Sometimes True   2 = Very True or Often True

0 1 2	1.	Acts too young for his/her age
0 1 2	2.	Allergy (describe): _____
		_____
0 1 2	3.	Argues a lot
0 1 2	4.	Asthma
0 1 2	5.	Behaves like opposite sex
0 1 2	6.	Bowel movements outside toilet
0 1 2	7.	Bragging, boasting
0 1 2	8.	Can't concentrate, can't pay attention for long
0 1 2	9.	Can't get his/her mind off certain thoughts; obsessions (describe): _____
0 1 2	10.	Can't sit still, restless, or hyperactive
0 1 2	11.	Clings to adults or too dependent
0 1 2	12.	Complains of loneliness
0 1 2	13.	Confused or seems to be in a fog
0 1 2	14.	Cries a lot
0 1 2	15.	Cruel to animals
0 1 2	16.	Cruelty, bullying, or meanness to others
0 1 2	17.	Day-dreams or gets lost in his/her thoughts
0 1 2	18.	Deliberately harms self or attempts suicide
0 1 2	19.	Demands a lot of attention
0 1 2	20.	Destroys his/her own things
0 1 2	21.	Destroys things belonging to his/her family or others
0 1 2	22.	Disobedient at home
0 1 2	23.	Disobedient at school
0 1 2	24.	Doesn't eat well
0 1 2	25.	Doesn't get along with other kids
0 1 2	26.	Doesn't seem to feel guilty after misbehaving
0 1 2	27.	Easily jealous
0 1 2	28.	Eats or drinks things that are not food — *don't* include sweets (describe): _____
		_____
0 1 2	29.	Fears certain animals, situations, or places, other than school (describe): _____
		_____
0 1 2	30.	Fears going to school

0 1 2	31.	Fears he/she might think or do something bad
0 1 2	32.	Feels he/she has to be perfect
0 1 2	33.	Feels or complains that no one loves him/her
0 1 2	34.	Feels others are out to get him/her
0 1 2	35.	Feels worthless or inferior
0 1 2	36.	Gets hurt a lot, accident-prone
0 1 2	37.	Gets in many fights
0 1 2	38.	Gets teased a lot
0 1 2	39.	Hangs around with others who get in trouble
0 1 2	40.	Hears sounds or voices that aren't there (describe): _____
		_____
0 1 2	41.	Impulsive or acts without thinking
0 1 2	42.	Would rather be alone than with others
0 1 2	43.	Lying or cheating
0 1 2	44.	Bites fingernails
0 1 2	45.	Nervous, highstrung, or tense
0 1 2	46.	Nervous movements or twitching (describe):
		_____
0 1 2	47.	Nightmares
0 1 2	48.	Not liked by other kids
0 1 2	49.	Constipated, doesn't move bowels
0 1 2	50.	Too fearful or anxious
0 1 2	51.	Feels dizzy
0 1 2	52.	Feels too guilty
0 1 2	53.	Overeating
0 1 2	54.	Overtired
0 1 2	55.	Overweight
	56.	Physical problems *without known medical cause:*
0 1 2		a. Aches or pains (*not* stomach or headaches)
0 1 2		b. Headaches
0 1 2		c. Nausea, feels sick
0 1 2		d. Problems with eyes (*not* if corrected by glasses) (describe): _____
0 1 2		e. Rashes or other skin problems
0 1 2		f. Stomachaches or cramps
0 1 2		g. Vomiting, throwing up
0 1 2		h. Other (describe): _____
		_____

Please see other side

Please Print

0 = Not True (as far as you know)   1 = Somewhat or Sometimes True   2 = Very True or Often True

0 1 2	57.	Physically attacks people	
0 1 2	58.	Picks nose, skin, or other parts of body (describe): _____
0 1 2	59.	Plays with own sex parts in public
0 1 2	60.	Plays with own sex parts too much
0 1 2	61.	Poor school work
0 1 2	62.	Poorly coordinated or clumsy
0 1 2	63.	Prefers being with older kids
0 1 2	64.	Prefers being with younger kids
0 1 2	65.	Refuses to talk
0 1 2	66.	Repeats certain acts over and over; compulsions (describe): _____
0 1 2	67.	Runs away from home
0 1 2	68.	Screams a lot
0 1 2	69.	Secretive, keeps things to self
0 1 2	70.	Sees things that aren't there (describe): _____
0 1 2	71.	Self-conscious or easily embarrassed
0 1 2	72.	Sets fires
0 1 2	73.	Sexual problems (describe): _____
0 1 2	74.	Showing off or clowning
0 1 2	75.	Shy or timid
0 1 2	76.	Sleeps less than most kids
0 1 2	77.	Sleeps more than most kids during day and/or night (describe): _____
0 1 2	78.	Smears or plays with bowel movements
0 1 2	79.	Speech problem (describe): _____
0 1 2	80.	Stares blankly
0 1 2	81.	Steals at home
0 1 2	82.	Steals outside the home
0 1 2	83.	Stores up things he/she doesn't need (describe): _____

0 1 2	84.	Strange behavior (describe): _____
0 1 2	85.	Strange ideas (describe): _____
0 1 2	86.	Stubborn, sullen, or irritable
0 1 2	87.	Sudden changes in mood or feelings
0 1 2	88.	Sulks a lot
0 1 2	89.	Suspicious
0 1 2	90.	Swearing or obscene language
0 1 2	91.	Talks about killing self
0 1 2	92.	Talks or walks in sleep (describe): _____
0 1 2	93.	Talks too much
0 1 2	94.	Teases a lot
0 1 2	95.	Temper tantrums or hot temper
0 1 2	96.	Thinks about sex too much
0 1 2	97.	Threatens people
0 1 2	98.	Thumb-sucking
0 1 2	99.	Too concerned with neatness or cleanliness
0 1 2	100.	Trouble sleeping (describe): _____
0 1 2	101.	Truancy, skips school
0 1 2	102.	Underactive, slow moving, or lacks energy
0 1 2	103.	Unhappy, sad, or depressed
0 1 2	104.	Unusually loud
0 1 2	105.	Uses alcohol or drugs for nonmedical purposes (describe): _____
0 1 2	106.	Vandalism
0 1 2	107.	Wets self during the day
0 1 2	108.	Wets the bed
0 1 2	109.	Whining
0 1 2	110.	Wishes to be of opposite sex
0 1 2	111.	Withdrawn, doesn't get involved with others
0 1 2	112.	Worries
	113.	Please write in any problems your child has that were not listed above:
0 1 2		_____
0 1 2		_____
0 1 2		_____

PLEASE BE SURE YOU HAVE ANSWERED ALL ITEMS

UNDERLINE ANY YOU ARE CONCERNED ABOUT.

Child Behavior Checklist/2-3

CHILD BEHAVIOR CHECKLIST FOR AGES 2-3

For office use only
ID #

CHILD'S NAME

PARENTS' USUAL TYPE OF WORK, even if not working now *(Please be specific — for example, auto mechanic, high school teacher, homemaker, laborer, lathe operator, shoe salesman, army sergeant.)*

SEX	AGE	ETHNIC GROUP OR RACE
☐ Boy ☐ Girl		

FATHER'S TYPE OF WORK: _____

MOTHER'S TYPE OF WORK: _____

TODAY'S DATE

Mo. _____ Date _____ Yr. _____

CHILD'S BIRTHDATE

Mo. _____ Date _____ Yr. _____

THIS FORM FILLED OUT BY:

☐ Mother (name): _____

Please fill out this form to reflect *your* view of the child's behavior even if other people might not agree. Feel free to write additional comments beside each item and in the space provided on page 2.

☐ Father (name): _____

☐ Other — name & relationship to child: _____

Below is a list of items that describe children. For each item that describes the child **now or within the past 2 months**, please circle the **2** if the item is **very true** or **often true** of the child. Circle the **1** if the item is **somewhat** or **sometimes true** of the child. If the item is **not true** of the child, circle the **0**. Please answer all items as well as you can, even if some do not seem to apply to the child.

0 = Not True (as far as you know)   **1 = Somewhat or Sometimes True**   **2 = Very True or Often True**

0 1 2	1. Aches or pains (without medical cause)	
0 1 2	2. Acts too young for age	
0 1 2	3. Afraid to try new things	
0 1 2	4. Avoids looking others in the eye	
0 1 2	5. Can't concentrate, can't pay attention for long	
0 1 2	6. Can't sit still or restless	
0 1 2	7. Can't stand having things out of place	
0 1 2	8. Can't stand waiting; wants everything now	
0 1 2	9. Chews on things that aren't edible	
0 1 2	10. Clings to adults or too dependent	
0 1 2	11. Constantly seeks help	
0 1 2	12. Constipated, doesn't move bowels	
0 1 2	13. Cries a lot	
0 1 2	14. Cruel to animals	
0 1 2	15. Defiant	
0 1 2	16. Demands must be met immediately	
0 1 2	17. Destroys his/her own things	
0 1 2	18. Destroys things belonging to his/her family or other children	
0 1 2	19. Diarrhea or loose bowels when not sick	
0 1 2	20. Disobedient	
0 1 2	21. Disturbed by any change in routine	
0 1 2	22. Doesn't want to sleep alone	
0 1 2	23. Doesn't answer when people talk to him/her	
0 1 2	24. Doesn't eat well (describe): _____	
0 1 2	25. Doesn't get along with other children	
0 1 2	26. Doesn't know how to have fun, acts like a little adult	
0 1 2	27. Doesn't seem to feel guilty after misbehaving	
0 1 2	28. Doesn't want to go out of home	
0 1 2	29. Easily frustrated	
0 1 2	30. Easily jealous	
0 1 2	31. Eats or drinks things that are not food — don't include sweets (describe): _____	
0 1 2	32. Fears certain animals, situations, or places (describe): _____	

0 1 2	33. Feelings are easily hurt	
0 1 2	34. Gets hurt a lot, accident-prone	
0 1 2	35. Gets in many fights	
0 1 2	36. Gets into everything	
0 1 2	37. Gets too upset when separated from parents	
0 1 2	38. Has trouble getting to sleep	
0 1 2	39. Headaches (without medical cause)	
0 1 2	40. Hits others	
0 1 2	41. Holds his/her breath	
0 1 2	42. Hurts animals or people without meaning to	
0 1 2	43. Looks unhappy without good reason	
0 1 2	44. Angry moods	
0 1 2	45. Nausea, feels sick (without medical cause)	
0 1 2	46. Nervous movements or twitching (describe): _____	
0 1 2	47. Nervous, highstrung, or tense	
0 1 2	48. Nightmares	
0 1 2	49. Overeating	
0 1 2	50. Overtired	
0 1 2	51. Overweight	
0 1 2	52. Painful bowel movements	
0 1 2	53. Physically attacks people	
0 1 2	54. Picks nose, skin, or other parts of body (describe): _____	
0 1 2	55. Plays with own sex parts too much	
0 1 2	56. Poorly coordinated or clumsy	
0 1 2	57. Problems with eyes without medical cause (describe): _____	
0 1 2	58. Punishment doesn't change his/her behavior	
0 1 2	59. Quickly shifts from one activity to another	
0 1 2	60. Rashes or other skin problems (without medical cause)	
0 1 2	61. Refuses to eat	
0 1 2	62. Refuses to play active games	
0 1 2	63. Repeatedly rocks head or body	
0 1 2	64. Resists going to bed at night	

0 = Not True (as far as you know)   1 = Somewhat or Sometimes True   2 = Very True or Often True

0	1	2	65. Resists toilet training (describe): _____	0	1	2	82.	Sudden changes in mood or feelings
			_____	0	1	2	83.	Sulks a lot
0	1	2	66. Screams a lot	0	1	2	84.	Talks or cries out in sleep
0	1	2	67. Seems unresponsive to affection	0	1	2	85.	Temper tantrums or hot temper
0	1	2	68. Self-conscious or easily embarrassed	0	1	2	86.	Too concerned with neatness or cleanliness
0	1	2	69. Selfish or won't share	0	1	2	87.	Too fearful or anxious
0	1	2	70. Shows little affection toward people	0	1	2	88.	Uncooperative
0	1	2	71. Shows little interest in things around him/her	0	1	2	89.	Underactive, slow moving, or lacks energy
0	1	2	72. Shows too little fear of getting hurt	0	1	2	90.	Unhappy, sad, or depressed
0	1	2	73. Shy or timid	0	1	2	91.	Unusually loud
0	1	2	74. Sleeps less than most children during day and/or night (describe): _____	0	1	2	92.	Upset by new people or situations (describe): _____
0	1	2	75. Smears or plays with bowel movements	0	1	2	93.	Vomiting, throwing up (without medical cause)
0	1	2	76. Speech problem (describe): _____	0	1	2	94.	Wakes up often at night
				0	1	2	95.	Wanders away from home
0	1	2	77. Stares into space or seems preoccupied	0	1	2	96.	Wants a lot of attention
0	1	2	78. Stomachaches or cramps (without medical cause)	0	1	2	97.	Whining
				0	1	2	98.	Withdrawn, doesn't get involved with others
0	1	2	79. Stores up things he/she doesn't need (describe): _____	0	1	2	99.	Worrying
							100.	Please write in any problems your child has that were not listed above.
0	1	2	80. Strange behavior (describe): _____	0	1	2		_____
				0	1	2		_____
0	1	2	81. Stubborn, sullen, or irritable	0	1	2		_____

PLEASE BE SURE YOU HAVE ANSWERED ALL ITEMS.   UNDERLINE ANY YOU ARE CONCERNED ABOUT.

Does your child have any illness, physical disability, or mental handicap? ☐ No ☐ Yes—Please describe

What concerns you most about your child?

Please describe the best things about your child:

Child Behavior Rating Form

INTERVIEWER CHILD BEHAVIOR RATING FORM

0 = not present   1= sometimes present   2= very often present

1. Complains of somatic problems
2. Easily frustrated
3. Difficulty concentrating or paying attention
4. Can't sit still, restless, or hyperactive
5. Constantly seeks help
6. Easily distracted by external stimuli
7. Nervous, highstrung, or tense
8. Underactive, slow moving, or lacks energy
9. Reluctant to talk about feelings
10. Lacks self-confidence
11. Leaves room during testing
12. Resistant or refuses to comply
13. Says "don't know" a lot
14. Wants to quit or does quit tasks
15. Works quickly and carelessly
16. Appears unhappy, sad, or depressed
17. Needs a great deal of encouragement, praise, or rewards
18. Gives up when having difficulty
19. Unconcerned about performance

Center for Epidemiologic Studies Depression Scale

CES-D SCALE

Below is a list of ways you may have felt during the past week. Please tell me how often you have felt this way during the past week:

   0. Rarely or none of the time
   1. Some or little of the time
   2. Occasionally or a moderate amount of time
   3. Most or all of the time

R	S	O	M

1. I was bothered by things that usually don't bother me.

R	S	O	M
0	1	2	3

2. I did not feel like eating; my appetite was poor.

R	S	O	M
0	1	2	3

3. I felt that I could not shake off the blues even with help from my family or friends.

R	S	O	M
0	1	2	3

4. I felt that I was just as good as other people.

R	S	O	M
0	1	2	3

5. I had trouble keeping my mind on what I was doing. 0

1	2	3

6. I felt depressed.

R	S	O	M
0	1	2	3

7. I felt that everything I did was an effort.

    0   1   2   3

8. I felt hopeful about the future.

    0   1   2   3

9. I thought my life had been a failure.

    0   1   2   3

10. I felt fearful.

    0   1   2   3

11. My sleep was restless.

    0   1   2   3

12. I was happy.

    0   1   2   3

13. I talked less than usual.

    0   1   2   3

14. I felt lonely.

    0   1   2   3

15. People were unfriendly.

    0   1   2   3

16. I enjoyed life.

    0   1   2   3

17. I had crying spells.

    0   1   2   3

18. I felt sad.

    0   1   2   3

19. I felt that people disliked me.

    0   1   2   3

20. I could not "get going."

    0   1   2   3

Taylor Manifest Anxiety Scale

TAYLOR MANIFEST ANXIETY SCALE

For each of the following statements, please tell me if it is true or false.

       True   False

1. I do not tire quickly.
      1   2

2. I am troubled by attacks of nausea.
      1   2

3. I believe that I am no more nervous than most others.
      1   2

4. I have very few headaches.
      1   2

5. I work under a great deal of tension.
      1   2

6. I cannot keep my mind on one thing.
      1   2

7. I worry over money and business.
      1   2

8. I frequently notice my hand shakes when I try to do something.
      1   2

9. I blush no more often than others.
      1   2

10. I have diarrhea once a month or more.
    1   2

11. I worry quite a bit over possible misfortune.
    1   2

12. I practically never blush.
    1   2

13. I am often afraid that I am going to blush.
    1   2

14. I have nightmares every few nights.
    1   2

15. My hands and feet are usually warm enough.
    1   2

16. I sweat very easily even on cool days.
    1   2

17. Sometimes when embarrassed, I break out in a sweat which
    annoys me greatly.
    1   2

18. I hardly ever notice my heart pounding and I am seldom short
    of breath.
    1   2

19. I feel hungry almost all the time.
    1   2

20. I am very seldom troubled by constipation.
    1   2

21. I have a great deal of stomach trouble.
    1   2

22. I have had periods in which I lost sleep over worry.
    1   2

23. My sleep is fitful and disturbed.
    1   2

24. I dream frequently about things that are best kept to myself.
    1   2

25. I am easily embarrassed.
    1   2

26. I am more sensitive than most other people.
    1   2

27. I frequently find myself worrying about something.
    1   2

28. I wish I could be as happy as others seem to be.
    1   2

29. I am usually calm and not easily upset.
    1   2

30. I cry easily.
    1   2

31. I feel anxiety about something or someone almost all the time.
    1   2

32. I am happy most of the time.
    1   2

33. It makes me nervous to have to wait.
    1   2

34. I have periods of such great restlessness that I cannot sit long in a chair.
    1   2

35. Sometimes I become so restless that I find it hard to get to sleep.
    1   2

36. I have sometimes felt that difficulties were piling up so high that I could not overcome them.
    1   2

37. I must admit that I have at times been worried beyond reason over something that did not matter.
    1   2

38. I have very few fears compared to my friends.
    1   2

39. I have been afraid of things or people that I knew could not hurt me.
    1   2

40. I certainly feel useless at times.
    1   2

41. I find it hard to keep my mind on a task or job.
    1   2

42. I am unusually self-conscious.
    1   2

43. I am inclined to take things hard.
    1   2

44. I am a high-strung person.
    1   2

45. Life is a strain for me much of the time.
    1   2

46. At times I think that I am no good at all.
    1   2

47. I am certainly lacking in self-confidence.
    1   2

48. Sometimes I feel that I am about to go to pieces.
    1   2

49. I shrink from facing a crisis or difficulty.
    1   2

50. I am entirely self-confident.
    1   2

Conflict Tactics Scale

CONFLICT TACTICS SCALE (CTS-STRAUS)

No matter how well a couple gets along, there are times when they disagree, get annoyed with the other person, or just have spats or fights because they're in a bad mood or tired or for some other reason. They also use many different ways of trying to settle their differences. I'm going to read you some things that different people do at times like this. As I read each item, please tell me about how many times a partner (boyfriend, husband, common-law husband, ex-partner) has used this approach with you in the past year.

1. Once
2. Twice
3. 3-5 times
4. 6-10 times
5. 11-20 times
6. More than 20 times
0. Never

1. Discussed an issue calmly

   1   2   3   4   5   6   0

2. Got information to back up his side of things

   1   2   3   4   5   6   0

3. Brought in, or tried to bring in, someone to help settle things

   1   2   3   4   5   6   0

4. Insulted or swore at you

   1   2   3   4   5   6   0

5. Sulked or refused to talk about an issue

    1   2   3   4   5   6   0

6. Stomped out of the room or house or yard

    1   2   3   4   5   6   0

7. Cried (when upset with you)

    1   2   3   4   5   6   0

8. Did or said something to spite you

    1   2   3   4   5   6   0

9. Threatened to hit or throw something at you

    1   2   3   4   5   6   0

10. Threw or smashed or hit or kicked something

    1   2   3   4   5   6   0

11. Threw something at you

    1   2   3   4   5   6   0

12. Pushed, grabbed, or shoved you

    1   2   3   4   5   6   0

13. Slapped you

    1   2   3   4   5   6   0

14. Kicked, bit, or hit you with a fist

    1   2   3   4   5   6   0

15. Hit or tried to hit you with something

    1   2   3   4   5   6   0

16. Beat you up

    1   2   3   4   5   6   0

17. Choked, strangled, or smothered you

    1   2   3   4   5   6   0

18. Threatened you with a knife or gun or automobile

    1   2   3   4   5   6   0

19. Used a knife or fired a gun

    1   2   3   4   5   6   0

20. Threatened your life in some other manner)

    1   2   3   4   5   6   0

21. Forced sex on you, or forced you to do a sexual thing you didn't want to

    1   2   3   4   5   6   0

In the past year, have any of the following happened and, if so, how often?

22. Did a partner ever physically fight with you in any other way, not mentioned above?

    1   2   3   4   5   6   0

23. Did you ever have injuries that showed, like bruises or scrapes, from something a partner did to you?

    1   2   3   4   5   6   0

24. Did you ever have other injuries, like broken bones or permanent injuries from something a partner did to you?

    1   2   3   4   5   6   0

Variable Clusters

Variable Clusters
1. Mother's Competence
   Educational Level
   Work History
   a. Occupation
   b. Salary
   c. Length of longest employment

2. Chronicity of Poverty
   Family of origin supported by welfare
   Total number of years family received Aid For Dependent
   Children
   Amount of time from first episode of homelessness until
   housed
   Number of moves past year
   Number of moves past five years

3. Child's Birth/Health Status
   Month mother began prenatal care
   Mother's use of drugs/alcohol during her pregnancy
   Infant hospitalization following birth
   Child has a chronic medical condition
   Mother's age at time of birth

4. Mother's History of Psychological Coping
   Psychiatric hospitalizations

Psychiatric medication
Suicide attempts
Amount of time mother has been clean and sober

5.   Mother's Current Psychological Functioning
Score on Center for Epidemiologic Studies Depression Scale
Score on Taylor Manifest Anxiety Scale

6.   Mother's Stressful Life Events as Child/Adolescent
Never knew one parent
Sent to live with relatives
Foster care placement
Parent's separated or divorced
Death of significant caregiver
Death of sibling
Maternal mental illness
Paternal mental illness
Maternal drug/alcohol use
Paternal drug/alcohol use
Mother serious physical illness
Father serious physical illness
Victim of physical abuse
Victim of sexual abuse
Witnessed domestic violence
Family fights
Mother served time in jail
Father served time in jail
Age left home to be on own
Age gave birth to first child

7.   Stressful Life Events as an Adult
Miscarriage
Abortion
Stillbirth
More than seven pregnancies
Surrendered a child for adoption
Infant death
Death of a parent
Death of a close friend
Loss/Separation from significant people
Serious medical condition

Involved with Child Protective Services
Child placed out of home
Convicted of a crime
Served more than one week in jail
Ever been on probation or parole

8. Mother's History of Victimization and Trauma
Victim of a violent crime
Ever been hit by a partner
Victim of battering past year
Victim of sexual abuse as child
Victim of physical abuse as child

9. Child's Stressful Life Events
Witnessed family violence
Sibling with a serious physical problem or emotional disorder
Four or more siblings
Less than two years spacing before next child
Never met father
Separated from mother for more than three months
Parents are separated
Mother views father negatively
Death of parent or significant caregiver
Maternal mental illness
Paternal mental illness
Mother abuses drugs or alcohol
Father abuses drugs or alcohol
Mother involved in criminal activity or has served time in jail
Father involved in criminal activity or has served time in jail
Family involved with Child Protective Services
Mother clean and sober less than one year
No or "Poor" relationship with father

10. School/Day Care
Amount of time spent in day-care
Amount of time spent at Head Start
Amount of time spent at a Therapeutic Nursery School
Amount of time spent in school

11. Natural Support Systems
Two caregivers in home
Father ever paid child support

Child sees father at least once a month
Number of important people in mother's life
Number of relatives mother is close to
Number of these relatives mother sees at least once a month
Number of close friends
Number of close friends mother sees at least once a month
Mother works or volunteers
Family attends church at least once a month

12. Agency Support
Mother has received counseling in past year
Mother attends a Day Treatment Program
Number of groups mother attends per month

Bibliography

Abernathy, V. (1973). Social network and response to the maternal role. *International Journal of Sociology and the Family, 3*, 86-92.

Achenbach, T.M. (1991). *Manual for the Child Behavior Checklist and revised child behavior profile.* Burlington, VT: Department of Psychiatry, University of Vermont.

Achenbach, T.M., & Edelbrock, C.S. (1981). Behavioral problems and competencies reported by parents of normal and disturbed children aged four through sixteen. *Monograph Society for Research on Child Development, 46* (1), 1-82.

Achenbach, T.M., & Edelbrock, C.S. (1983). *Manual for the Child Behavior Checklist and revised child behavior profile.* Burlington, VT: University Associates in Psychiatry.

Achenbach, T.M., Edelbrock, C.S., & Howell, C.T. (1987). Empirically based assessment of the behavioral/emotional problems of 2-3-year-old children. *Journal of Abnormal Child Psychology, 15*, 629-650.

Ainsworth, M.D.S. (1972). Attachment and dependency: A comparison. In J.L. Gewirtz (Ed.), *Attachment and dependency*, (pp. 97-137). Washington, D.C.: Winston.

Ainsworth, M.D.S. (1982). Attachment: Retrospect and prospect. In C.M. Parkes & J. Stevenson-Hinde (Eds.), *The place of attachment in human behavior*, (pp. 3-30) New York: Basic Books.

Ainsworth, M.D.S., Bell, S.M., & Stayton, D.J. (1971). Individual differences in strange-situation behavior of one-year-olds. In H.A. Schaffer (Ed.), *The origins of human social relations*, (pp. 17-57). London: Academic Press.

Alperstein, G., Rappaport, C., & Flanigan, J.M. (1988). Health problems of homeless children in New York City. *American Journal of Public Health, 78*, 1232-1233.

Amott, T.L. (1990). Black women and AFDC: Making entitlement out of necessity. In L. Gordon (Ed.), *Women, the state, and welfare*, (pp. 280-298). Madison, WI: University of Wisconsin Press.

Anderson, S.C., Boe, T., & Smith, S. (1988). Homeless women. *Affilia, 3*, (2), 62-70.

Anthony, E.J. (1974). The syndrome of the psychologically vulnerable child. In E.J. Anthony & C. Koupernick (Eds.), *The child in his family, Vol. 3: Children at psychiatric risk*, (pp. 3-10). New York: Wiley.

Anthony, E.J. (1974). The syndrome of the psychologically invulnerable child. In E.J. Anthony & C. Koupernick (Eds.), *The child in his family, Vol. 3: Children at psychiatric risk*, (pp. 529-544). New York: Wiley.

Anthony, E.J. (1987). Risk, vulnerability, and resilience: An overview. In E.J. Anthony & B.J. Cohler (Eds.), *The invulnerable child*, (pp. 3-48). New York: Guilford.

Anthony, E.J., & Cohler, B.J. (Eds.). (1987). *The invulnerable child*. New York: Guilford.

Appley, M.H., & Trumbull, R. (1967). *Psychological stress*. New York: Appleton-Century-Crofts.

Arend, R., Gove, F.L., & Sroufe, L.A. (1979). Continuity of individual adaption from infancy to kindergarten: A predictive study of ego resiliency and curiosity in pre-schoolers. *Child Development, 50*, 950-959.

Ball, R.E. (1986). Marriage: Conducive to greater life satisfaction for American black women? In R. Staples (Ed.), *The black family:Essays and studies*, (pp. 146- 154). Belmont, CA: Wadsworth.

Bandler, L.S. (1967). Family functioning: A psychosocial perspective. In C.A. Malone, E. Pavenstedt, I. Mattick, L.S. Bandler, M.R. Stein, & N.L. Mintz (Eds.), *The drifters: Children of disorganized lower-class families*, (pp. 225-253).

Barnes, E.J. (1972). The black community as a source of positive self-concept for black children: A theoretical perspective. In R. Jones (Ed.), *Black psychology*, (pp. 166-192). New York: Harper & Row.

Barnes, G.E., & Prosen, H. (1985). Parental death and depression. *Journal of Abnormal Psychology, 94*, 64-69.

Bassuk, E.L. (1986). Homeless families: Single mothers and their children in Boston shelters. *New Directions for Mental Health Services, 30*, 45-53.

Bassuk, E.L., & Rosenberg, L. (1988). Why does family homelessness occur? A case-control study. *American Journal of Public Health, 78* (7), 783-788.

Bassuk, E.L., & Rosenberg, L. (1990). Psychosocial characteristics of homeless children and children without homes. *Pediatrics, 85* (3), 257-261.

Bassuk, E.L., & Rubin, L. (1987). Homeless children: A neglected population. *American Journal of Orthopsychiatry, 57* (2), 279-286.

Bassuk, E.L., Rubin, L., & Lauriat, A. (1984). Is homelessness a mental health problem? *American Journal of Psychiatry, 141,* 1546-1550.

Bassuk, E.L., Rubin, L., & Lauriat, A. (1986). Characteristics of sheltered homeless families. *American Journal of Public Health, 76* (9), 1097-1101.

Baumann, D., & Grigsby, C. (1988). *Understanding the homeless: From research to action.* Austin: University of Texas.

Beck, A.T, Rush, A.J., Shaw, B.F., & Emery, G. (1979). *Cognitive therapy of depression.* New York: Guilford.

Beck, A.T., Ward, C.H., Mendelson, M., Mock, J., & Erbaugh, J. (1961). An inventory for measuring depression. *Archives of General Psychiatry, 4,* 561-571.

Bee, H.L., Barnard, K.E., Eyres, S.J., Gray, C.A., Hammond, M.A., Spietz, A.L., Snyder, C., & Clark, B. (1982). Prediction of IQ and language skill from perinatal status, child performance, family characteristics, and mother-infant interaction. *Child Development, 53,* 1134-1156.

Bee, H.L., Hammond, M.A., Eyres, S.J., Barnard, K.E., & Snyder, C. (1986). The impact of parental life change on the early development of children. *Research in Nursing and Health, 9,* 65-74.

Belle, D. (Ed.). (1982). *Lives in stress: Women and depression.* Beverly Hills: Sage Publications.

Belle, D. (1983). The impact of poverty on social networks and supports. *Marriage and Family Review, 5,* 89-103.

Belle, D. (1984). Inequality and mental health: Low-income and minority women. In L. Walker (Ed.), *Women and mental health policy,* (pp. 135-150). Beverly Hills, CA: Sage Publications.

Belsky, J. (1980). Child maltreatment: An ecological integration. *American Psychologist, 35,* 320-335.

Benedek, T. (1956). Psychobiological aspects of mothering. *American Journal of Orthopsychiatry, 26,* 272-278.

Berezin, J. (1988). *Promises to keep: Child care for New York City's homeless children.* New York: Child Care, Inc.

Bernard, S.E. (1966). The economic and social adjustment of low-income female-headed families. *Dissertation Abstracts International, 27,* (5-A), 1458.

Bishop, J. (1977). *Jobs, cash transfers, and marital instability: A review of the evidence.* Madison: University of Wisconsin Institute for Research on Poverty.

Bleuler, M. (1978). *The schizophrenic disorders: Long-term patient and family studies.* New Haven, CT: Yale University Press.

Block, J. (1971). *Lives through time.* Berkeley, CA: Bancroft Books.

Block, J.H., & Block, J. (1980). The role of ego control and ego-resiliency in the organization of behavior. In W.A. Collins (Ed.), *Development of cognition, affect, and social relations: The Minnesota Symposia on Child Psychology, Vol. 13,* (pp. 39-101). Hillsdale, NJ: Lawrence Erlbaum.

Bower, T.G. (1977). *A primer of infant development.* San Francisco, CA: W.H. Freeman.

Bowlby, J. (1969). *Attachment and loss: Vol. 1. Attachment.* New York: Basic Books.

Bowlby, J. (1973). *Attachment and loss: Vol. 2. Separation, anxiety, and anger.* New York: Basic Books.

Bowlby, J. (1979). The making and breaking of affectional bonds. *British Journal of Psychiatry, 131,* 201-210.

Boxill, N.A. (1989, October 4). *Examining the homeless situation of children.* Testimony presented before the Subcommittee on Children, Family, Drugs and Alcoholism of the Committee on Labor and Human Resources United States Senate. Washington, D.C.: U.S. Government Printing Office.

Boxill, N.A., & Beaty, A.L. (1990). Mother/child interaction among homeless women and their children in a public night shelter in Atlanta, Georgia. *Child and Youth Services, 14,* 49-64.

Boyd-Franklin, N. (1989). *Black families in therapy: A multisystems approach.* New York: Guilford.

Bretherton, I. (1985). Attachment theory: Retrospect and prospect. In I. Bretherton & E. Waters (Eds.), *Growing points in attachment theory and research. Monographs for the Society for Research in Child Development, 50,* 3-38.

Brody, G.H., & Forehand, R. (1986). Maternal perceptions of child maladjustment as a function of the combined influence of child behavior and maternal depression. *Journal of Consulting and Clinical Psychology, 54* (2) 237-240.

Broman, S., Nichols, R., & Kennedy, W. (1975). *Preschool IQ: Prenatal and early developmental correlates.* Hillsdale, NJ: Lawrence Erlbaum.

Bronfenbrenner, U. (1986). Ecology of the family as a context for human development: Research perspectives. *Developmental Psychology, 22* (6), 723-742.

Bronfenbrenner, U., & Crouter, A.C. (1982). Work and family through time and space. In S.B. Kamerman & C.D. Hayes (Eds.), *Families that work: Children in a changing world*. Washington, D.C.: National Academy Press.

Brown, B., & Rosenbaum, L. (1984). Stress and competence. In J.H. Humphrey (Ed.), *Stress in childhood*, (pp. 127-154). New York: AMS Press.

Brown, D.R., & Gary, L.E. (1987). Stressful life events, social support networks, and physical and mental health of urban black adults. *Journal of Human Stress, 13*, 165-174.

Brown, D.R., & Gary, L.E. (1988). Unemployment and psychological distress among black American women. *Sociological Focus, 21*, 209-220.

Brown, G.W., Bhrolchain, M.N., & Harris, T. (1975). Social class and psychiatric disturbance among women in an urban population. *Sociology, 9*, 225-254.

Brown, G.W., & Harris, T. (1978). *Social origins of depression: A study of psychiatric disorder in women*. London: Tavistock Publications.

Brown, K.S., & Ziefert, M. (1990). A feminist approach to working with homeless women. *Affilia, 5* (1), 6-20.

Browne, A. (1993). Family violence and homelessness: The relevance of trauma histories in the lives of homeless women. *American Journal of Orthopsychiatry, 63* (3), 370-384.

Buckner, J.C., Bassuk, E.L., & Zima, B.T. (1993). Mental health issues affecting homeless women: Implications for intervention. *American Journal of Orthopsychiatry, 63*, 385-399.

Burnam, M.A., Stein, J.A., Golding, J.M., Siegel, J.M., Sorenson, S.B., Forsythe, A.B., & Telles, C.A. (1998). Sexual assault and mental disorders in a community population. *Journal of Consulting and Clinical Psychology, 56*, 843-850.

Buss, T., & Redburn, F.S. (1983). *Mass unemployment: Plant closings and community mental health*. Beverly Hills, CA: Sage.

Cazenave, N., & Straus, M. (1979). Race, class, network embeddedness, and family violence: A search for potent support systems. *Journal of Comparative Family Studies, 10*, 281-300.

Center for the Study of Social Policy (1986). The "flip-side" of black families headed by women: The economic status of black men. In R. Staples (Ed.), *The black family: Essays and studies*, (pp. 232-238). Belmont, CA: Wadsworth.

Chasnoff, I.J., Burns, W.J., Schnoll, S.H., & Burns, K.A. (1985). Cocaine use in pregnancy. *The New England Journal of Medicine, 313*, 666-669.

Chasnoff, I.J., Schnoll, S.H., Burns, W.J., & Burns, K.A. (1984). Maternal nonnarcotic substance abuse during pregnancy: Effects on infant development. *Neurobehavioral Toxicology and Teratology, 6,* 277-280.

Children's Defense Fund (1991). *Child poverty in America.* Washington, D.C.: Author.

Children's Defense Fund (1991). *Homeless families: Failed policies and young victims.* Washington, D.C.: Author.

Christensen, A., Phillips, S., Glasgow, R.E., & Johnson, S.M. (1983). Parental characteristics and interactional dysfunction in families with child behavior problems: A preliminary investigation. *Journal of Abnormal Child Psychology, 11,* 153-166.

Cicirelli, U.G. (1976). Siblings helping siblings. In V.L. Allen (Ed.), *Children as tutors.* New York: Academic Press.

Citizens Committee for Children (1988). *Children in storage: Families in New York City's barracks-style shelters.* New York: Author.

Clark, R. (1983). *Family life and school achievement: Why poor black children succeed or fail.* Chicago: University of Chicago Press.

Cochran, M.M., & Brassard, J.A. (1979). Child development and personal social networks. *Child Development, 50,* 601-616.

Cohen, L.J. (1974). The operational definition of human attachment. *Psychological Bulletin, 81* (4), 207-217.

Cohen, S., Glass, D.C., & Singer, J.E. (1973). Apartment noise, auditory discrimination, and reading ability in children. *Journal of Experimental Social Psychology, 9,* 407-422.

Cohen, S., & Wills, T.A. (1985). Stress, social support, and the buffering hypothesis. *Psychological Bulletin, 98,* 310-357.

Colletta, N. (1981). Social support and the risk of maternal rejection by adolescent mothers. *Journal of Psychology, 109,* 191-197.

Collins, A., & Pancoast, D. (1976). *National helping networks.* Washington, D.C.: National Association of Social Workers.

Coopersmith, S. (1967). *The antecedents of self-esteem.* San Francisco: Freeman.

Coppolillo, H.P. (1987). Organizing diagnostic data: Models of the parents, ego psychology, and topography. In H.P. Coppolillo (Ed.), *Psychodynamic psychotherapy of children,* (pp. 147-173). Madison: International Universities Press.

Coro Foundation (1991). *There's no place called home: A needs assessment of homeless children in shelters in Alameda County.* Alameda County: Author.

Cotterell, J.L. (1986). Work and community influences on the quality of child rearing. *Child Development, 57*, 362-374.

Cramer, B., & Stern, D.N. (1988). Evaluation of changes in mother-infant brief psychotherapy: A single case study. *Infant Mental Health Journal, 9* (1), 20-45.

Crnic, K.A. & Greenberg, M.T. (1987). Maternal stress, social support, and coping: Influences on the early mother-child relationship. In C. Boukydis (Ed.), *Research on support for parents and infants in the postnatal period* (pp. 25-40). Norwood, New Jersey: Ablex.

Crnic, K.A., Greenberg, M.T., Ragozin, A.S., Robinson, N.M., & Basham, R.B. (1983). Effects of stress and social support on mothers and premature and full-term infants. *Child Development, 54*, 209-219.

Crnic, K.A., Greenberg, M.T., Robinson, N.M., & Ragozin, A.S. (1984). Maternal stress and social support: Effects on the mother-infant relationship from birth to eighteen months. *American Journal of Orthopsychiatry, 54*, 224-235.

Crockenberg, S. (1981). Infant irritability, mother responsiveness, and social support influences on the security of infant-mother attachment. *Child Development, 52*, 857-865.

Crockenberg, S. (1987). Support for adolescent mothers during the postnatal period: Theory and research. In C. Boukydis (Ed.), *Research on support for parents and infants in the postnatal period*, (pp. 3-24). Norwood, NJ: Ablex.

Crystal, S. (1984). Homeless men and women: The gender gap. *Urban and Social Change Review, 17*, 2-6.

Cummings, E.M., & Zahn-Waxler, C., & Radke-Yarrow, M. (1981). Young children's responses to expressions of anger and affection by others in the family. *Child Development, 52* (4), 1274-1282.

Dahlstrom, W.G., & Welsh, G.S. (1960). *An MMPI handbook: A guide to use in clinical practice and research.* Minneapolis, MN: University of Minnesota Press.

Daniel, J., Hampton, R., & Newberger, E. (1983). Child abuse and accidents in black families: A controlled comparative study. *American Journal of Orthopsychiatry, 53*, 645-653.

D'Ercole, A., & Struening, E. (1990). Victimization among homeless women: Implications for service delivery. *Journal of Community Psychology, 18*, 141-152.

Devins, G.M., & Orme, C.M. (1985). Center for Epidemiologic Studies Depression Scale. In D.J. Keyser & R.C. Sweetland (Eds.), *Test Critiques*, Vol. II, pp. 144-160.

Diamant, A. (1986, May 18). Teen-age pregnancy and the black family. *The Boston Globe*, magazine.

Dixon, S.D., & Bejar, R. (1989). Echoencephalographic findings in neonates associated with maternal cocaine and methamphetamine use: Incidence and clinical correlates. *The Journal of Pediatrics, 115,* 770-778.

Donahue, P.J., & Tuber, S.B. (1995). The impact of homelessness on children's level of aspiration. *Bulletin of the Menninger Clinic, 59* (2), 249-255.

Dow-Edwards, D.L. (1988). Developmental effects of cocaine. In D. Clovet, K. Asghar, & R. Brown (Eds.), *Mechanisms of cocaine abuse and toxicity,* (pp. 290-303). (NIDA Research Monograph 88), Department of Health and Human Services: National Institute of Drug Abuse, Division of Preclinical Research.

Downey, G. & Coyne, J. (1990). Children of depressed parents: An integrative review. *Psychological Bulletin, 108,* 50-76.

Dressler, W. (1985). Extended family relationships, social support, and mental health in a southern black community. *Journal of Health and Social Behavior, 26,* 39-48.

Duncan, G.J., & Rodgers, W.L. (1988). Longitudinal aspects of childhood poverty. *Journal of Marriage and the Family, 50,* 1007-1021.

Dunn, J., Kendrick, C., & MacNamee, R. (1981). The reaction of first-born children to the birth of a sibling: Mothers' reports. *Journal of Child Psychology and Psychiatry, 22,* 1-18.

Easterbrooks, M.A., & Lamb, M.E. (1979). The relationship between quality of infant-mother attachment and infant competence in initial encounters with peers. *Child Development, 50,* 380-387.

Egeland, B., & Kreutzer, T. (1991). A longitudinal study of the effects of maternal stress and protective factors on the development of high-risk children. In E.M. Cummings, A.L. Greene, & K.H. Karraker (Eds.), *Life-span developmental psychology: Perspectives on stress and coping,* (pp. 61-83). Hillsdale, NJ: Lawrence Erlbaum.

Elder, G. (1974). *Children of the great Depression.* Chicago: University of Chicago Press.

Elder, G. (1979). Historical change in life patterns and personality. In P. Baltes & O. Brim (Eds.), *Life span development and behavior,* (Vol. 2, pp. 117-159). New York: Academic Press.

Ellwood, D.T. (1988). *Poor support.* New York: Basic Books.

Emergency Services Network of Alameda County (1990). *Homelessness in Oakland: 1990 Composite profiles and unduplicated count.* Oakland: Author.

Erikson, E.H. (1950). *Childhood and society.* New York: Norton.

Erikson, E.H. (1964). *Childhood and society.* New York: Norton.

Estroff, T.W., Herrera, C., Gaines, R., Shaffer, D., Gould, M. & Green, A.H. (1984). Maternal psychopathology and perception of child behavior in psychiatrically referred and child maltreatment families. *Journal of American Academy of Child and Adolescent Psychiatry, 23,* 649-652.

Felsman, J.K., & Vaillant, G.E. (1987). Resilient children as adults: A 40-year study. In E.J. Anthony & B.J. Cohler (Eds.), *The invulnerable child,* (pp. 289-314). New York: Guilford.

Fenichel, O. (1945). *Neurotic acting out, Collected papers, Vol. 2.* New York: Norton.

Fergusson, D.M., Horwood, L.J., Gretten, M.E., & Shannon, F.J. (1985). Family life events, maternal depression, and maternal and teacher descriptions of child behavior. *Pediatrics, 75,* 30-35.

Finkelhor, D. (1983). Common features of family abuse. In D. Finkelhor, R.J. Gelles, G.T. Hotaling, & M.A. Straus (Eds.), *The dark side of families: Current family violence research,* (pp. 17-28). Beverly Hills, CA: Sage.

Finkelhor, D. & Browne, A. (1985). The traumatic impact of child sexual abuse: A conceptualization. *American Journal of Orthopsychiatry, 55,* 530-541.

Finkelhor, D., Gelles, R.J., Hotaling, G.T., & Straus, M.A. (Eds.) (1983). *The dark side of families: Current family violence research.* Beverly Hills, CA: Sage.

Finnegan, L.P., Mellott, J.M., Ryan, L.M., & Wapner, R.J. (1989). Perinatal exposure to cocaine: Human studies. In J.M. Lakoski, M.P. Galloway, & F.J. White (Eds.), *Cocaine: Pharmacology, physiology, and cultural strategies,* (pp. 391-409). Florida: CRC Press.

Fischer, P. (1984). *Health and social characteristics of Baltimore homeless persons.* Paper presented at the meeting of the American Psychological Association, Toronto.

Forehand, R., Wells, K.C., McMahon, R.J., Griest, D., & Rogers, T. (1982). Maternal perceptions of maladjustment in clinic-referred children: An extension of earlier research. *Journal of Behavioral Assessment, 4,* 145-151.

Fox, S.J., Barrnett, R.J., Davies, M., & Bird, H.R. (1990). Psychopathology and developmental delay in homeless children: A pilot study. *Journal of the American Academy of Child and Adolescent Psychiatry, 29* (5), 732-735.

Fraiberg, S., Adelson, E., & Shapiro, V. (1980). Ghosts in the nursery: A psychoanalytic approach to the problems of impaired infant-mother relationships. In S. Fraiberg (Ed.), *Clinical studies in infant mental health: The first year of life,* (pp. 164-196). New York: Basic Books.

Franklin, D.L. (1988). The impact of early childbearing on developmental outcomes: The case of black adolescent parenting. *Family Relations, 37,* 268-274.

Friedlander, S., Weiss, D.S., & Traylor, J. (1986). Assessing the influence of maternal depression on the validity of the Child Behavior Checklist. *Journal of Abnormal Child Psychology, 14,* 123-133.

Fulmer, R.H. (1987). Special problems of mourning in low-income single-parent families. In M. Lindblad-Goldberg (Ed.), *Clinical issues in single-parent households,* (pp. 19-37). Rockville, MD: Aspen Publishers, Inc.

Furstenberg, F., & Brooks-Gunn, J. (1987). *Adolescent mothers later in life.* Cambridge: Cambridge University Press.

Furstenberg, F., & Crawford, A. (1978). Family support: Helping teenage mothers to cope. *Family Planning Perspectives, 10,* 322-333.

Galambos, N., & Silbereisen, R. (1987). Income change, parental outlook, and adolescent expectations for job success. *Journal of Marriage and the Family, 49,* 141-149.

Garbarino, J. (1976). A preliminary study of some ecological correlates of child abuse: The impact of socioeconomic stress on mothers. *Child Development, 47,* 178-185.

Garbarino, J., Kostelny, K., & Dubrow, N. (1991). What children can tell us about living in danger. *American Psychologist, 46* (4), 376-383.

Garcia-Coll, C., Vohr, B., Hoffman, J., & Oh, W. (1986). Maternal and environmental factors affecting developmental outcome of infants of adolescent mothers. *Journal of Developmental and Behavioral Pediatrics, 7,* 230-236.

Gardner, E.A. (1968). *Development of a symptom checklist for the measurement of depression in a population.* Unpublished data.

Garfinkel, I., & McLanahan, S. (1986). *Single mothers and their children: A new American dilemma.* Washington, D.C.: Urban Institute Press.

Garmezy, N. (1971). Vulnerability research and the issue of primary prevention. *American Journal of Orthopsychiatry, 41* (1), 101-116.

Garmezy, N. (1974). The study of competence in children at risk for severe psychopathology. In E.J. Anthony & C. Koupernik (Eds.), *The child in his family: Children at psychiatric risk,* (Vol. 3). New York: Wiley.

Garmezy, N. (1976). Vulnerable and invulnerable children: Theory, research, and intervention. *Catalog of selected documents in psychology, 6,* 96.

Garmezy, N. (1981). Children under stress: Perspectives on antecedents and correlates of vulnerability and resistance to psychopathology. In A.I. Rabin, J. Aronoff, A.M. Barclay, & R.A. Zucker (Eds.), *Further explorations in personality,* (pp. 196-269). New York: Wiley.

Garmezy, N. (1983). Stressors of childhood. In N. Garmezy & M. Rutter (Eds.), *Stress, coping, and development in children*, (pp. 43-84). New York: McGraw-Hill.

Garmezy, N. (1985). Stress resistant children: The search for protective factors. In J.E. Stevenson (Ed.), *Recent research in developmental psychopathology* (Book supplement to the Journal of Child Psychology and Psychiatry, No.4, pp. 213-233). New York: Pergamon Press.

Garmezy, N. (1987). Stress, competence, and development: Continuities in the study of schizophrenic adults, children vulnerable to psychopathology, and the search for stress-resistant children. *American Journal of Orthopsychiatry*, *57*, 159-174.

Garmezy, N., & Masten, A.S. (1991). The protective role of competence indicators in children at risk. In E.M. Cummings, A.L. Greene, & K.H. Karraker (Eds.), *Life-span developmental psychology: Perspectives on stress and coping*, (pp. 151-174). Hillsdale, NJ: Lawrence Erlbaum.

Garmezy, N., Masten, A.S., & Tellegen, A. (1984). The study of stress and competence in children: A building block for developmental psychopathology. *Child Development*, *55*, 97-111.

Garmezy, N., & Tellegen, A. (1984). Studies of stress-resistant children: Methods, variables, and preliminary findings. In F.J. Morrison, C. Lore, & D.P. Keating (Eds.), *Applied Developmental Psychology*, Vol. 1, (pp. 231-287). London: Academic Press.

Gecas, V. (1979). The influence of social class on socialization. In W. Burr, R. Hill, F. Nye, & I. Reiss (Eds.), *Contemporary theories about the family: Research-based theories*, (Vol. 1, pp. 365-404). New York: Free Press.

Gelles, R.J. (1973). Child abuse as psychopathology: A sociological critique and reformulation. *American Journal of Orthopsychiatry*, *43*, 611-621.

Gelles, R.J. (1980). Violence in the family: A review of research in the seventies. *Journal of Marriage and the Family*, *42*, 143-155.

George, C., & Solomon, J. (1989). Internal working models of caregiving and security of attachment at age six. *Infant Mental Health Journal*, *10* (3), 222-237.

Gewirtz, J.L. (1972). *Attachment and dependency*. Washington, D.C.: Winston.

Gewirtz, J.L. (1976). The attachment acquisition process as evidenced in the maternal conditioning of cued infant responding. *Human Development*, *19*, 143-155.

Gewirtzman, R., & Fodor, I. (1987). The homeless child at school: From welfare hotel to classroom. *Child Welfare*, *66*, 236-245.

Gil, D. (1970). *Violence against children: Physical abuse in the United States*. Cambridge: Harvard University Press.

Gil, D. (1971). Violence against children. *Journal of Marriage and the Family,* *33,* 637-657.

Gil, D. (1979). *Child abuse and violence.* New York: AMS Press.

Giovannoni, J., & Billingsley, A. (1970). Child neglect among the poor: *f* study of parental adequacy in families of three ethnic groups. *Child Welfare, 49,* 196-204.

Gocka, E. (1965). *American Lake norms for 200 MMPI scales.* Unpublished manuscript, Veterans Administration Hospital, American Lake, WA.

Goodban, N. (1985). The psychological impact of being on welfare. *Social Service Review, 59,* 403-422.

Goodman, L.A. (1991a). The prevalence of abuse among homeless and housed poor mothers: A comparison study. *American Journal of Orthopsychiatry, 61* (4), 489-500.

Goodman, L.A. (1991b). The relationship between social support and family homelessness: A comparison study of homeless and housed mothers. *Journal of Community Psychology, 19,* 321-332.

Goodman, L.A., Saxe, L., & Harvey, M. (1991). Homelessness as psychological trauma. *American Psychologist, 46* (11), 1219-1225.

Gotlib, I.H., & Cane, D.B. (1989). Self-report assessment of depression and anxiety. In P.C. Kendall & D. Watson (Eds.), *Anxiety and depression: Distinctive and overlapping features,* (pp. 131-169). San Diego: Academic Press.

Griest, D.L., Forehand, R., Wells, K.C., & McMahon, R.J. (1980). An examination of differences between nonclinic and behavior-problem-clinic- referred children and their mothers. *Journal of Abnormal Psychology, 89,* 497- 500.

Griest, D.L., Wells, K.C., & Forehand, R. (1979). An examination of predictors of maternal perceptions of maladjustment in clinic-referred children. *Journal of Abnormal Psychology, 88,* 271-281.

Grigsby, C., Baumann, D., Gregorich, S.E., & Roberts-Gray, C. (1990). Disaffiliation to entrenchment: A model for understanding homelessness. *Journal of Social Issues, 46* (4), 141-156.

Grinker, R.R. (1968). Psychiatry and our dangerous world. In *Psychiatric research in our changing world.* Proceedings of an International Symposium, Montreal.

Grossman, P. (1979). Prematurity, poverty-related stress, and the mother-infant relationship. *Dissertation Abstracts International, 40,* (4-B).

Gruenberg, E.M. (1981). Risk factor research methods. In National Institute of Mental Health, *Risk factor research in the major mental disorders* (DHHS Publication No. 81-1068, pp. 8-19). Washington, D.C.: U.S. Government Printing Office.

Gunnar, M.R., Mangelsdorf, S., Kestenbaum, R., Lang, S., Larson, M., & Andreas, D. (1989). Stress and coping in early development. In D. Cicchetti (Ed.), *The emergence of a discipline: Rochester symposium on developmental psychopathology*, (pp. 119-138). Hillsdale, NJ: Lawrence Erlbaum.

Guttentag, M., Salasin, S., & Belle, D. (1980). *The mental health of women.* New York: Academic Press.

Hagen, J.L. (1987). Gender and homelessness. *Social Work, 32*, 312-316.

Hagen, J.L., & Ivanoff, A.M. (1988). Homeless women: A high-risk population. *Affilia, 3* (1), 19-33.

Hall, J.A., & Maza, P.L. (1990). No fixed address: The effects of homelessness on families and children. *Child and Youth Services, 14* (1), 35-47.

Hammen, C. (1991). Parent-child relationships and depression. In C. Hammen (Ed.), *Depression runs in families: The social context of risk and resilience in children of depressed mothers*, (pp. 140-172). New York: Springer-Verlag.

Hausman, B., & Hammen, C. (1993). Parenting in homeless families: The double crisis. *American Journal of Orthopsychiatry, 63* (3), 358-369.

Hazen, N.L., & Durrett, M.E. (1982). Relationship of security of attachment to exploration and cognitive mapping abilities in two-year-olds. *Developmental Psychology, 18* (5), 751-759.

Height, D.I. (1985). What must be done about children having children. *Ebony*, pp. 76-84.

Heinicke, C.M., Beckwith, L., & Thompson, A. (1988). Early intervention in the family system: A framework and review. *Infant Mental Health Journal, 9*, 111-141.

Henderson, S., Byrne, D.G., & Duncan-Jones, P. (1981). *Neurosis and the social environment.* Sydney: Academic Press.

Herman, J. (1992). *Trauma and recovery.* New York: Basic Books.

Herman, J., & Hirschman, L. (1977). Father-daughter incest. *Signs, 2*, 1-22.

Herrenkohl, E.C., Herrenkohl, R.C., & Toedter, L.J. (1983). Perspectives on the intergenerational transmission of abuse. In D. Finkelhor, R.J. Gelles, G.T. Hotaling, & M.A. Straus (Eds.), *The dark side of families: Current family violence research*, (pp. 305-316). Beverly Hills, CA: Sage.

Hetherington, E.M. (1980). Children and divorce. In R. Henderson (Ed.), *Parent- child interaction: Theory, research, and prospect*, (pp. 33-58). New York: Academic Press.

Hetherington, E.M. (1984). Stress and coping in children and families. In A.B. Doyle, D. Gold, & D.S. Moskowitz (Eds.), *Children in families under stress*, (pp. 7-33). San Francisco: Jossey-Bass.

Hilgard, E.R., Jones, L.V., & Kaplan, S.J. (1951). Conditioned discrimination as related to anxiety. *Journal of Experiential Psychology, 42*, 94-99.

Hill, R.B. (1972). *Strengths of black families*. New York: Emerson Hall.

House, J.S., Landis, K.R., & Umberson, D. (1988). Social relationships and health. *Science, 241*, 540-545.

Howard, J. (1989). Cocaine and its effects on the newborn. *Developmental Medicine and Child Neurology, 31* (2) 255-257.

Howard, J., Beckwith, L., Rodning, C., & Kropenske, V. (1989). The development of young children of substance-abusing parents: Insights from seven years of intervention and research. *Zero to Three, 9* (5), 8-17.

Hughes, H.M. (1982). Brief interventions with children in a battered women's shelter: A model preventive program. *Family Relations, 31*, 495-502.

Hughes, H.M., & Barad, S.J. (1982). Changes in the psychological functioning of children in a battered women's shelter: A pilot study. *Victimology, 7* (1-4), 60-68.

Hughes, M., & Demo, D.H. (1989). Self perceptions of black Americans: Self-esteem and personal efficacy. *American Journal of Sociology, 95*, 132-159.

Hughes, H.M., Parkinson, D., & Vargo, M. (1987, August). *Witnessing spouse abuse and experiencing physical abuse: A "double whammy"?* Paper presented at the annual meeting of the American Psychological Association, New York.

Hunter, R., & Kilstrom, N. (1979). Breaking the cycle in abusive families. *American Journal of Psychiatry, 136*, 1320-1322.

Institute of Medicine (1988). *Homelessness, health, and human needs*. Washington, D.C.: National Academy Press.

Jaffe, P.G., Wolfe, D.A., & Wilson, S.K. (1990). *Children of battered women*. Newbury Park, CA: Sage.

Janoff-Bulman, R., & Frieze, I.H. (1983). A theoretical perspective for understanding reactions to victimization. *Journal of Social Issues, 39* (2), 1-17.

Jenkins, S., & Diamond, B. (1985). Ethnicity and foster care: Census data as predictors of placement variables. *American Journal of Orthopsychiatry, 55*, 267-276.

Jordan, J. (1987). *Clarity in connection: Empathic knowing, desire, and sexuality* (Work in Progress, No. 29). Wellesley, MA: Stone Center Working Paper Series.

Kalish, R.A., & Knudtson, F.W. (1976). Attachment versus disengagement: A life-span conceptualization. *Human Development, 19*, 171-181.

Kauffman, C., Grunebaum, H., Cohler, B., & Garner, E. (1979). Superkids: Competent children of psychotic mothers. *American Journal of Psychiatry, 136* (11), 1398-1402.

Kellam, S.G., Ensminger, M.E., & Turner, R.J. (1977). Family structure and the mental health of children: Concurrent and longitudinal community-wide studies. *Archives of General Psychiatry, 34*, 1012-1022.

Keltner, B. (1990). Family characteristics of preschool social competence among black children in a Head Start program. *Child Psychiatry and Human Development, 21* (2), 95-108.

Kempe, C.H., & Helfer, R.E. (1972). *Helping the battered child and his family.* Philadelphia, PA: J.B. Lippincott.

Kessler, R.C., & McLeod, J.D. (1985). Social support and mental health in community samples. In S. Cohen & S.L. Syme (Eds.), *Social support and health*, (pp. 219-240). San Diego, CA: Academic Press.

Kobasa, S. (1979). Personality and resistance to illness. *American Journal of Community Psychology, 7*, 413-423.

Kohut, H. (1977). *The restoration of the self.* New York: International Universities Press, Inc.

Koplow, L. (1996). Why homeless children can't sit still. In L. Koplow (Ed.), *Unsmiling faces: How preschoolers can heal*, (pp. 219-230). New York: Teachers College Press.

Kopp, C.B. (1983). Risk factors in development. In P.H. Mussen (Ed.), *Handbook of Child Psychology, Vol. 2: Infancy and developmental psychology*, (pp.1081-1188). New York: Wiley.

Kopp, C.B., & Kaler, S.R. (1989). Risk in infancy: Origins and implications. *American Psychologist, 44* (2), 224-230.

Kopp, C.B., & Krakow, J.B. (1983). The developmentalist and the study of biological risk: A view of the past with an eye toward the future. *Child Development, 54* (5), 1086-1108.

Lamb, M.E. (1978). Interactions between eighteen-month-olds and their preschool-aged siblings. *Child Development, 49*, 51-59.

Lewis, M., Feiring, C., McGuffog, C., & Jaskir, J. (1984). Predicting psychopathology in six-year-olds from early social relations. *Child Development, 55*, 123-136.

Lewis, M.R., & Meyers, A.F. (1989). The growth and development status of homeless children entering shelters in Boston. *Public Health Reports, 104,* 247-250.

Liem, R., & Liem, J. (1978). Social class and mental illness reconsidered: The role of economic stress and social support. *Journal of Health and Social Behavior, 19,* 139-156.

Lindblad-Goldberg, M. (1987). The assessment of social networks in black, low- income, single-parent families. In M. Lindblad-Goldberg (Ed.), *Clinical issues in single-parent households,* (pp. 39-46). Rockville, MD: Aspen Publishers.

Lindblad-Goldberg, M., & Dukes, J. (1985). Social support in black, low-income, single-parent families: Normative and dysfunctional patterns. *American Journal of Orthopsychiatry, 55* (1), 42-58.

Livneh, H., & Redding, C.A. (1986). A factor analytic study of manifest anxiety: A transsituational, trans-temporal investigation. *The Journal of Psychology, 120* (3), 253-263.

Luthar, S.S., & Zigler, E. (1991). Vulnerability and competence: A review of research on resilience in childhood. *American Journal of Orthopsychiatry, 61* (1), 6-22.

Lyons-Ruth, K., Botein, S., & Grunebaum, H.U. (1984). Reaching the hard-to-reach: Serving isolated and depressed mothers with infants in the community. In B. Cohler & J. Musick (Eds.), *Interventions with psychiatrically disabled parents and their young children,* (pp. 95-122). San Francisco: Jossey-Bass.

Maden, M. & Wrench, D. (1977). Significant findings in child abuse research. *Victimology, 11,* 196-224.

Mahler, M., Pine, F., & Bergman, A. (1975). *The psychological birth of the human infant.* New York: Basic Books.

Main, M., & Goldwyn, R. (1984). Predicting rejection of her infant from mother's representation of her own experiences: A preliminary report. *International Journal of Child Abuse and Neglect, 8,* 203-217.

Main, M., Kaplan, N., & Cassidy, J. (1985). Security in infancy, childhood, and adulthood: A move to the level of representation. In I. Bretherton & E. Waters (Eds.), *Growing points in attachment theory and research. Monographs for the Society for Research in Child Development, 50* (1-2, Serial No. 209), 66-104.

Makosky, V.P. (1982). Sources of stress: Events or conditions? In D. Belle (Ed.), *Lives in stress: Women and depression,* (pp. 35-53). Beverly Hills, CA: Sage.

Malson, M. (1983). The social support systems of Black families. *Marriage and Family Review, 5* (4), 37-57.

Marshall, N. (1982). The public welfare system: Regulation and dehumanization. In D. Belle (Ed.), *Lives in stress: Women and depression,* (pp. 96-108). Beverly Hills, CA: Sage.

Masten, A.S. (1989). Resilience in development: Implications of the study of successful adaptation for developmental psychopathology. In D. Cicchetti (Ed.), *The emergence of a discipline: Rochester symposium on developmental psychopathology,* (pp. 261-294). Hillsdale, NJ: Lawrence Erlbaum.

Masten, A.S., & Garmezy, N. (1985). Risk, vulnerability, and protective factors in developmental psychopathology. In B.B. Lahey, & A.E. Kazdin (Eds.), *Advances in clinical child psychology, Vol. 8,* (pp. 1-52). New York: Plenum.

Masten, A.S., Miliotis, D., Graham-Bermann, S.A., Ramirez, M.L., & Neeman, J. (1993). Children in homeless families: Risks to mental health development. *Journal of Consulting and Clinical Psychology, 61* (2), 335-343.

Masten, A.S., Morison, P., Pellegrini, D., & Tellegen, A. (1990). Competence under stress: Risk and protective factors. In J. Rolf, A.S. Masten, D. Cicchetti, K.H. Neuchterlein, & S. Weintraub (Eds.), *Risk and protective factors in the development of psychopathology,* (pp. 236-256). Cambridge: Cambridge University Press.

Matas, L., Arend, R., & Sroufe, L.A. (1978). Continuity of adaption in the second year: The relationship between quality of attachment and later competence. *Child Development, 49,* 547-556.

McAdoo, H. (1979, May). Black kinship. *Psychology Today,* pp. 67-110.

McChesney, K.Y. (1987). *Characteristics of the residents of two inner-city emergency shelters for the homeless.* Los Angeles: University of Southern California, Social Science Research Institute.

McChesney, K.Y. (1988). *Absence of a family safety net for homeless families.* Paper submitted to Sociology of Family Session, American Sociological Association.

McChesney, K.Y. (1991). Macroeconomic issues in poverty: Implications for child and youth homelessness. In J.H. Kryder-Coe, L.M. Salamon, & J. M. Molnar (Eds.), *Homeless children and youth,* (pp. 143-173). New Brunswick, NJ: Transactions Publishers.

McGee, R., Williams, S., & Kaskani, J. (1983). Prevalence of self-reported depressive symptoms and associated social factors of mothers in Donedin. *British Journal of Psychiatry, 143,* 473-479.

McLanahan, S.S., & Booth, K. (1989). Mother-only families: Problems, prospects, and politics. *Journal of Marriage and the Family, 51,* 557-580.

McLoyd, V.C. (1989). Socialization and development in a changing economy: The effects of parental job and income loss on children. *American Psychologist, 44,* 293-302.

McLoyd, V.C. (1990). The impact of economic hardship on black families and children: Psychological distress, parenting, and socioemotional development. *Child Development, 61,* 311-346.

McLoyd, V.C., & Wilson, L. (1990). Maternal behavior, social support, and economic conditions as predictors of psychological distress in children. In V.C. McLoyd & C. Flanagan (Eds.), *New Directions for Child Development, Economic stress: Effects on family and child development, 46,* (pp. 49-69). San Francisco: Jossey-Bass.

Meiselman, K. (1978). *Incest.* San Francisco: Jossey-Bass.

Meisels, S.J. (1989). Can developmental screening tests identify children who are developmentally at-risk? *Pediatrics, 83,* 578-585.

Melnick, V.L., & Williams, C.S. (1987). *Children and families without homes: Observations from thirty case studies.* Washington, D.C.: University of the District of Columbia, Center for Applied Research and Urban Policy.

Mihaly, L. (1991). Beyond the numbers: Homeless families and children. In J.H. Kryder-Coe, L.M. Salamon, & J.M. Molnar (Eds.), *Homeless children and youth,* (pp. 11-31). New Brunswick, NJ: Transactions Press.

Milburn, N., & D'Ercole, A. (1991). Homeless women: Moving toward a comprehensive model. *American Psychologist, 46* (11), 1161-1169.

Miller, J.B. (1988). *Connections, disconnections, and violations* (Work in Progress, No. 33). Wellesley, MA: Stone Center Working Paper Series.

Mills, C., & Ota, H. (1989). Homeless women with minor children in the Detroit metropolitan area. *Social Work, 34,* 485-489.

Molnar, J. (1991). Introduction. In J.H. Kryder-Coe, L.M. Salamon, & J.M. Molnar (Eds.), *Homeless children and youth,* (pp. 3-9). New Brunswick, N.J.: Transaction Publishers.

Molnar, J., Klein, T., Knitzer, J., & Ortiz-Torres, B. (1988). *Home is where the heart is: The crisis of homeless children and families in New York City.* New York: Bank Street College of Education (ERIC Document Reproduction Service No. ED 304-228).

Molnar, J., & Rath, W. (1990, August). *Beginning at the beginning: Public policy and homeless children.* Paper presented at the 98th Annual Convention of the American Psychological Association, Boston.

Molnar, J., Rath, W.R., & Klein, T.P. (1990). Constantly compromised: The impact of homelessness on children. *Journal of Social Issues, 46* (4), 109-124.

Molnar, J., Rath, W.R., Klein, T.P., Lowe, C., & Hartmann, A.H. (1991). *Ill fares the land: The consequences of homelessness and chronic poverty for children and families in New York City.* New York: Bank Street College of Education.

Molnar, J., & Rubin, D.H. (1991, March). *The impact of homelessness on children: Review of prior studies and implications for future research.* Paper presented at the NIMH/NIAAA research conference organized by The Better Homes Foundation, Cambridge, MA.

Mowbray, C., Solarz, A., Johnson, S.V., Phillips-Smith, E., & Combs, C.J. (1986). *Mental health and homelessness in Detroit: A research study.* Lansing: Michigan Department of Mental Health.

Murphy, L.B. (1962). *The widening world of childhood: Paths toward mastery.* New York: Basic Books.

Murphy, L.B. (1987). Further reflections on resilience. In E.J. Anthony & B.J. Cohler (Eds.), *The invulnerable child,* (pp. 84-105). New York: Guilford.

Murphy, L.B., & Moriarty, A.E. (1976). *Vulnerability, coping, and growth.* New Haven: Yale University Press.

Murphy, L.B., & Moriarty, A.E. (1978). *Vulnerability, coping, and growth: From infancy to adolescence* (2nd edition). New Haven: Yale University Press.

Myers, B.J., Britt, G.C., Lodder, D.E., Kendall, K.A., & Williams-Peterson, M.G. (1992). Effects of cocaine exposure on infant development: A review. *Journal of Child and Family Studies, 1* (4) 393-415.

Myers, H.F. (1982). Research on the Afro-American family: A critical review. In B.A. Bass, G.E. Wyatt, & G.J. Powell (Eds.), *The Afro-American family: Assessment, treatment, and research issues,* (pp. 35-68). New York: Grune & Stratton.

Myers, H.F., & King, L.M. (1983). Mental health issues in the development of the Black American child. In G.J. Powell, J. Yamamoto, A. Romero, & A. Morales (Eds.), *The psychosocial development of minority group children,* (pp. 275-306). New York: Bruner-Mazel.

Myers, J.K., & Weissman, M.M. (1980). Use of self-report symptom scale to detect depression in a community sample. *American Journal of Psychiatry, 137,* 1081-1084.

National Black Child Development Institute, Inc. (1989). *Who will care when parents can't? A study of black children in foster care.* New York: Urban Research Center, New York University.

Neiman, L. (1988). A critical review of resiliency literature and its relevance to homeless children. *Children's Environments Quarterly, 5* (1), 17-25.

Neuspiel, D.R., Hamel, S.C. (1991). Cocaine and infant behavior. *Journal of Developmental and Behavioral Pediatrics, 12,* 55-64.

Newson, J., & Newson, E. (1963). *Infant care in an urban community.* London: Allen & Unwin.

Nuechterlein, K. (1970). *Competent disadvantaged children: A review of the research.* Unpublished honor's thesis, University of Minnesota, Minneapolis.

Nyamathi, A., & Vasquez, R. (1989). Impact of poverty, homelessness, and drugs on Hispanic women at risk for HIV infection. *Hispanic Journal of Behavioral Sciences, 11* (4), 299-314.

O'Connor, J.P., Lorr, M., & Stafford, J.W. (1956). Some patterns of manifest anxiety. *Journal of Clinical Psychology, 12,* 160-163.

O'Dougherty, M., & Wright, F.S. (1989). Children born at medical risk: Factors affecting vulnerability and resilience. In. J. Rolf, A.S. Masten, D. Cicchetti, K.H. Nuechterlein, & S. Weintraub (Eds.), *Risk and protective factors in the development of psychopathology,* (pp. 120-180). Cambridge: Cambridge University Press.

O'Grady, D., & Metz, R. (1987). Resilience in children at high risk for psychological disorder. *Journal of Pediatric Psychology, 12* (1), 3-23.

Oro, A.S., & Dixon, S.D. (1987). Perinatal cocaine and methamphetamine exposure: Maternal and neonatal correlates. *The Journal of Pediatrics, 11,* 571-578.

Parke, R.D. (1978). Children's home environments: Social and cognitive effects. In I. Altman & J.F. Wohlwill (Eds.), *Children and the environment, Vol. 3,* (pp. 33-81). New York: Plenum.

Parker, G., Cowen, E.L., Work, W.C., & Wyman, P.A. (1990). *Test correlates of stress-resilience among urban school children.* Manuscript submitted for publication.

Parker, G., & Hazdi-Pavlovic, D. (1984). Modification of levels of depression in mother-bereaved women by parental and marriage relationships. *Psychological Medicine, 14,* 125-135.

Parker, S., Greer, S., & Zuckerman, B. (1988). Double jeopardy: The impact of poverty on early child development. In B. Zuckerman, M. Weitzman, & J. Alpert (Eds.), *Pediatric clinics of North America, 35* (6), 1227-1240.

Pasamanick, B., & Knobloch, H. (1960). Brain damage and reproductive casualty. *American Journal of Orthopsychiatry, 30,* 298-305.

Pascoe, J., Loda, F., Jeffries, V., & Earp, J. (1981). The association between mothers' social support and provision of stimulation to their children. *Journal of Developmental Behavioral Pediatrics*, 2, 15-19.

Patterson, G. (1988). Stress: A change agent for family process. In N. Garmezy & M. Rutter (Eds.), *Stress, coping, and development in children*, (pp. 235-264). Baltimore: Johns Hopkins University Press.

Patterson, G., DeBaryshe, B., & Ramsey, E. (1989). A developmental perspective on antisocial behavior. *American Psychologist*, *44* (2), 329-335.

Pavenstedt, E. (Ed.) (1967). *The drifters: Children of disorganized lower-class families*. Boston: Little, Brown.

Pearlin, L., & Johnson, J. (1977). Marital status, life strains, and depression. *American Sociological Review*, *42*, 704-715.

Pearlin, L.I., Lieberman, M.A., Menaghan, E.G., & Mullan, J.T. (1981). The stress process. *Journal of Health and Social Behavior*, *22*, 337-356.

Pianta, R.C., Egeland, B., & Sroufe, L.A. (1990). Maternal stress and children's development: Prediction of school outcomes and identification of protective factors. In J. Rolf, A.S. Masten, D. Cicchetti, K.H. Nuechterlein, & S. Weintraub (Eds.), *Risk and protective factors in the development of psychopathology*, (pp. 215-235). Cambridge: Cambridge University Press.

Pines, M. (1979, Jan.). Superkids. *Psychology Today*, pp. 53-63.

Porter, B., & O'Leary, K.D. (1980). Marital discord and childhood behavior problems. *Journal of Abnormal Child Psychology*, *8*, 287-295.

Powell, G.J. (1983). Coping with adversity: The psychosocial development of Afro-American children. In G.J. Powell, J. Yamamoto, A. Romero, & A. Morales (Eds.), *The psychosocial development of minority group children*,(pp. 49-76). New York: Bruner-Mazel.

Proshansky, H.M., & Gottlieb, N.M. (1989). The development of place identity in the child. *Zero to Three*, *10* (2), 18-25.

Provence, S. (1974). Some relationships between activity and vulnerability in the early years. In E.J. Anthony & C. Koupernik (Eds.), *The child in his family, Vol. 3: Children at psychiatric risk*, (pp. 157-166). New York: Wiley.

Quinton, D. (1980). Family life in the inner city: Myth and reality. In M. Marland (Ed.), *Education for the inner city*. London: Heinemann Educational.

Rachman, S.J. (1979). The concept of required helpfulness. *Behavior Research and Therapy*, *17*, 1-6.

Radke-Yarrow, M., & Sherman, T. (1990). Hard growing: Children who survive. In J. Rolf, A.S. Masten, D. Cicchetti, K.H. Neuchterlein, & S. Weintraub (Eds.), *Risk and protective factors in the development of psycho- pathology*, (pp. 97-119). Cambridge: Cambridge University Press.

Radloff, L. (1975). Sex differences in depression: The effects of occupation and marital status. *Sex Roles, 1*, 249-266.

Radloff, L.S. (1977). The CES-D scale: A new self-report depression scale for research in the general population. *Applied Psychological Measurement, 1*, 385-401.

Rafferty, Y., & Shinn, M. (1991). The impact of homelessness on children. *American Psychologist, 46* (11), 1170-1179.

Raskin, A., Schulterbrandt, J., Reating, W., & McKeon, J. (1969). Replication of factors of psychopathology in interview, ward behavior, and self-report ratings of hospitalized depressives. *Journal of Nervous and Mental Disease, 198*, 87-96.

Ray, S.A., & McLoyd, V.C. (1986). Fathers in hard times: The impact of unemployment and poverty on paternal and marital relations. In M. Lamb (Ed.), *The father's role*, (pp. 339-383). New York: Wiley.

Redmond, S.P., & Brackmann, J. (1990). Homeless children and their caretakers. In J. Momeni (Ed.), *Homelessness in the United States: Vol. 2. Data and Issues*, (pp. 123-132). Westport, CT: Greenwood.

Rescorla, L., Parker, R., & Stolley, P. (1991). Ability, achievement, and adjustment in children. *American Journal of Orthopsychiatry, 61* (2), 210-220.

Reyes, L.M., & Waxman, L.D. (1989). *A status report on hunger and homelessness in America's cities, 1989: A 27-city survey.* Washington, D.C.: U.S. Conference of Mayors.

Rickard, K.M., Forehand, R., Wells, K.C., Griest, D.L., & McMahon, R.J. (1981). A comparison of mothers of clinic-referred deviant, clinic-referred nondeviant, and nonclinic children. *Behavior Research and Therapy, 19*, 201-205.

Ricks, M. (1985). The social transmission of parental behavior: Attachment across generations. In I. Bretherton & E. Waters (Eds.), *Growing points of attachment theory and research. Monographs of the Society for Research in Child Development, 50* (1-2, Serial No. 209) 211-227.

Rivlin, L.G. (1990). Home and homelessness in the lives of children. *Child and Youth Services, 14* (1), 5-17.

Roberts, R.E., & Vernon, S.W. (1983). The Center for Epidemiologic Studies Depression Scale: Its use in a community sample. *American Journal of Psychiatry, 140*, 41-46.

Rog, D.J., Holupka, C.S., & McCombs-Thorton, K.L. (1995). Implementation of the homeless families program: Service models and preliminary outcomes. *American Journal of Orthopsychiatry, 65*, (4) 502-513.

Rog, D.J., McCombs-Thorton, K.L., Gilbert-Mongelli, A.M., Brito, M.C., & Holupka, C.S. (1995). Implementation of the homeless families program: Characteristics, strengths, and needs of participant families. *American Journal of Orthopsychiatry, 65* (4) 514-528.

Rolf, J. (1972). The social and academic competence of children vulnerable to schizophrenia and other pathologies: Current status. *Journal of Abnormal Psychology, 80*, 225-243.

Rollins, B., & Thomas, D. (1979). Parental support, power, and control techniques in the socialization of children. In W. Burr, R. Hill, F. Nye, & I. Reiss, (Eds.), *Contemporary theories about the family: Research-based theories, Vol. 1*, (pp. 317-364). New York: Free Press.

Rosenbaum, A. & O'Leary, K.D. (1981). Children: The unintended victims of marital violence. *American Journal of Orthopsychiatry, 51* (4), 692-699.

Rossi, P.H., Wright, J.D., Fisher, G.A., & Willis, G. (1987). The urban homeless: Estimating composition and size. *Science, 235*, 1336-1341.

Roy, K. (1950). Parents' attitudes toward their children. *Journal of Home Economics, 42*, 652-653.

Rutter, M. (1970). Sex differences in children's responses to family stress. In E.J. Anthony & C. Koupernik (Eds.), *The child in his family, Vol. 1*, (pp. 165-196). New York: Wiley.

Rutter, M. (1971). Parent-child separation: Psychological effects on children. *Journal of Child Psychology and Psychiatry, 12*, 233-260.

Rutter, M. (1978). Early sources of security and competence. In J.S. Bruner & A. Garten (Eds.), *Human growth and development*, (pp. 3-21). London: Oxford University Press.

Rutter, M. (1979). Protective factors in children's responses to stress and disadvantage. In M.W. Kent & J.E. Rolf (Eds.), *Primary prevention of psychopathology, Vol. 3* (pp. 49-74). Hanover, NH: University Press of New England.

Rutter, M. (1981). Social/emotional consequences of day care for pre-school children. *American Journal of Orthopsychiatry, 51*, 4-28.

Rutter, M. (1981). Stress, coping and development: Some issues and some questions. *Journal of Child Psychology and Psychiatry, 22* (4) 323-356.

Rutter, M. (1982). Epidemiological-longitudinal approaches to the study of development. In W.A. Collins (Ed.), *Minnesota Symposia on Child Psychology, Vol. 15: The concept of development*, (pp. 105-144). Hillsdale, NJ: Lawrence Erlbaum.

Rutter, M. (1983). Stress, coping, and development: Some issues and some questions. In N. Garmezy & M. Rutter (Eds.), *Stress, coping, and development in children*, (pp. 1-41). New York: McGraw-Hill.

Rutter, M. (1984). Continuities and discontinuities in socioemotional development: Empirical and conceptual perspectives. In R. Emde & R. Harmon (Eds.), *Continuities and discontinuities in development*, (pp. 41-68). New York: Plenum.

Rutter, M. (1985). Resilience in the face of adversity: Protective factors and resistance to psychiatric disorder. *British Journal of Psychiatry, 147*, 598-611.

Rutter, M. (1987). Psychosocial resilience and protective mechanisms. *American Journal of Orthopsychiatry, 57* (3), 316-331.

Rutter, M. (1990). Psychosocial resilience and protective mechanisms. In J. Rolf, A.S. Masten, D. Cicchetti, K.H. Neuchterlein, & S. Weintraub (Eds.), *Risk and protective factors in the development of psychopathology*, (pp. 181- 214). New York: Cambridge University Press.

Rutter, M., Cox, A., Tupling, C., Berger, M., & Yule, W. (1975). Attainment and adjustment in two geographical areas: I. The prevalence of psychiatric disorder. *British Journal of Psychiatry, 126*, 493-509.

Rutter, M., Maughan, B., Mortimore, P., Ouston, J., & Smith, A. (1979). *Fifteen thousand hours: Secondary schools and their effects on children.* Cambridge, MA: Harvard University Press.

Rutter, M., Quinton, D., & Yule, B. (1977). *Family pathology and disorder in children.* London: Wiley.

Rutter, M., Yule, B., Quinton, D., Rowlands, O., Yule, W., & Berger, M. (1975). Attainment and adjustment in two geographical areas: II. Some factors accounting for area differences. *British Journal of Psychiatry, 126*, 520-533.

Saegert, S. (1981). Environment and children's mental health: Residential destiny and low income children. In A. Baum & J.E. Singer (Eds.), *Handbook of psychology and health, Vol. 2*, (pp. 247-271). Hillsdale, NJ: Lawrence Erlbaum.

Sameroff, A.J., Barocas, R., & Seifer, R. (1984). The early development of children born to mentally-ill women. In N.F. Watt, E.J. Anthony, L.C. Wynne, & J. Rolf (Eds.), *Children at risk for schizophrenia: A longitudinal perspective*, (pp. 482-514). Cambridge, England: Cambridge University Press.

Sameroff, A.J., & Chandler, M.J. (1975). Reproductive risk and the continuum of caretaking casualty. In F.D. Horowitz, M. Hetherington, S. Scarr-Salapatek, & G. Siegel (Eds.), *Review of Child Development Research, Vol. 4*, (pp. 187-243). Chicago: University of Chicago Press.

Sameroff, A.J., & Seifer, R. (1983). Familial risk and child competence. *Child Development, 54*, 1254-1268.

Sameroff, A.J., & Seifer, R. (1990). Early contributors to developmental risk. In J. Rolf, A.S. Masten, D. Cicchetti, K.H. Neuchterlein, & S. Weintraub (Eds.), *Risk and protective factors in the development of psychopathology*, (pp. 52-66). Cambridge, England: Cambridge University Press.

Sameroff, A.J., Seifer, R., Barocas, R., Zax, M., & Greenspan, S. (1987). Intelligence quotient scores of four-year-old children: Social-environmental risk factors. *Pediatrics, 79* (3), 343-350.

Sandler, L.W. (1975). Infant and caretaking environment: Investigation and conceptualization of adaptive behavior in a system of increasing complexity. In E.J. Anthony (Ed.), *Explorations in Child Psychiatry*, (pp. 129-166). New York: Plenum.

Sandler, I.N., & Block, M. (1979). Life stress and maladaptation of children. *American Journal of Community Psychology, 7* (4), 425-440.

Sandler, I.N., & Block, M. (1980). Life stresses and maladjustment of poor children. *American Journal of Community Psychology, 8*, 41-52.

Sandler, I.N., Miller, P., Short, J., & Wolchik, S. (1989). Social support as a protective factor for children in stress. In D. Belle (Ed.), *Children's social networks and social supports*, (pp. 277-307). New York: Wiley.

Sattler, J.M. (1990). *Assessment of children*. San Diego, CA: Sattler.

Schaffer, H.R., & Emerson, P.E. (1964). The development of social attachments in infancy. *Society for Research in Child Development, Monograph No. 94, 29* (3), 1-77.

Schaughency, E.A., & Lahey, B.B. (1985). Mothers and fathers perceptions of child deviance: Roles of child behavior, parental depression, and marital satisfaction. *Journal of Consulting and Clinical Psychology, 53*, 718-723.

Schulz, D.A. (1977). *Coming up Black: Patterns of ghetto socialization*. Englewood Cliffs, NJ: Prentice Hall.

Seifer, R., & Sameroff, A.J. (1987). Multiple determinants of risk and invulnerability. In E.J. Anthony & B.J. Cohler (Eds.), *The invulnerable child*, (pp. 51-69). New York: Guilford.

Seligman, M.E.P. (1975). *Helplessness: On depression, development, and death*. San Francisco: W.H. Freeman.

Seligman, M.E.P. (1978). Comment and integration. *Journal of Abnormal Psychology, 87*, 165-179.

Shinn, M., Knickman, J.R., & Weitzman, B.C. (1991). Social relationships and vulnerability to becoming homeless among poor families. *American Psychologist, 46* (11), 1180-1187.

Shonkoff, J. (1982). Biologic and social factors contributing to mild mental retardation. In K. Heller, W. Holtzman, & S. Messiuk (Eds.), *Placing children in special education: A strategy for equity*, (pp. 133-181). Washington, D.C.: National Academy Press.

Smith, E. (1991). *Patterns of alcoholism in subsamples of the homeless.* Unpublished raw data.

Solarz, A., & Bogat, G.A. (1990). When social support fails: The homeless. *Journal of Community Psychology, 18*, 79-96.

Sosin, M.R., Colson, P., & Grossman, S. (1988). *Homelessness in Chicago: Poverty and pathology, social institutions, and social change.* Chicago: University of Chicago, School of Social Service Administration.

Spinetta, J., & Rigler, D. (1972). The child abusing parent: A psychological review. *Psychological Bulletin, 77*, 296-304.

Spitz, R. (1957). *No and yes: On the genesis of human communication.* New York: International Universities Press.

Sroufe, L.A., & Fleeson, J. (1986). Attachment and the construction of relationships. In W.W. Hartup & Z. Rubin (Eds.), *Relationships and development*, (pp. 51-72). Hillsdale, NJ: Lawrence Erlbaum.

Stack, C. (1970). *All our kin: Strategies for survival in a black community.* New York: Harper & Row.

Staples, R. (1986). Changes in black family structure: The conflict between family ideology and structural conditions. In R. Staples (Ed.), *The black family: Essays and studies*, (pp. 20-28). Belmont, CA: Wadsworth.

Stayton, D.J., & Ainsworth, M.D.S. (1973). Individual differences in infant responses to brief everyday separations as related to other infant and maternal behaviors. *Developmental Psychology, 9*, 226-23.

Steinberg, L., Catalano, R., & Dooley, D. (1981). Economic antecedents of child abuse and neglect. *Child Development, 52*, 975-985.

Stern, D.N., Hofer, L., Haft, W., & Dore, J. (1985). Affect attunement: The sharing of feeling states between mother and infant by means of inter-modal fluency. In T. Field & N. Fox (Eds.), *Social perception in infants*, (pp. 249-268). Norwood, NJ: Ablex.

Stiver, I.P. (1990a). *Dysfunctional families and wounded relationships, Part I.* (Work in Progress, No. 41). Wellesley, MA: Stone Center Working Paper Series.

Stiver, I.P. (1990b). *Dysfunctional families and wounded relationships, Part II.* (Work in Progress, No. 44). Wellesley, MA: Stone Center Working Paper Series.

Straus, M.A. (1979). Measuring intrafamily conflict and violence: The conflict tactics (CT) scales. *Journal of Marriage and the Family, 41,* 75- 88.

Straus, M.A., Gelles, R.J., & Steinmetz, S.K. (1980). *Behind closed doors: Violence in the American family.* New York: Doubleday/Anchor.

Sullivan, H.S. (1953). *The interpersonal theory of psychiatry.* New York: Norton.

Taylor, J.A. (1953). A personality scale of manifest anxiety. *Journal of Abnormal and Social Psychology, 48* (2), 285-290.

Taylor, R.J. (1988). Structural determinants of religious participation among Black Americans. *Review of Religious Research, 30,* 114-125.

Taylor, R.J., Chatters, L.M., Tucker, M.B., & Lewis, E. (1991). Developments in research on Black families: A decade review. In A. Booth (Ed.), *Contemporary families: Looking forward, looking back,* (pp. 275-296). Minneapolis: National Council on Family Relations.

Thomas, A., Chess, S, & Birch, H. (1968). *Temperament and behavior disorders in children.* New York: New York University.

Thomas, A., Chess, S., Birch, H., Hertzig, M., & Korn, S. (1963). *Behavioral individuality in early childhood.* New York: New York University.

Thompson, M.S., & Ensminger, M.E. (1989). Psychological well-being among mothers with school-age children: Evolving family structures. *Social Forces, 67,* 715-730.

Thompson, R. (1982). Stability of infant-mother attachment and its relationship to changing life circumstances in an unselected middle class sample. *Child Development, 53,* 144-148.

Thompson, R.A., & Lamb, M.E. (1983). Security of attachment and stranger sociability in infancy. *Developmental Psychology, 19,* 184-191.

Thompson, R.A., Lamb, M.E., & Estes, D. (1982). Stability of infant-mother attachment and its relationship to changing life circumstances in an unselected middle-class sample. *Child Development, 53* (1), 144-148.

Trickett, P., & Susman, E. (1988). Parental perceptions of child-rearing practices in physically-abusive and non-abusive families. *Developmental Psychology, 24,* 270-276.

U.S. Conference of Mayors. (1993). *A status report on hunger and homelessness in America's cities: A 26-city survey.* Washington, D.C.: Author.

Van Dyke, D.C., & Fox, A.A. (1990). Fetal drug exposure and its possible implications for learning in the preschool and school-age population. *Journal of Learning Disabilities, 23* (3), 160-162.

Vaughan, B., Egeland, B., Sroufe, L.A., & Waters, E. (1979). Individual differences in the infant-mother attachment at 12 and 18 months: Stability and change in families under stress. *Child Development, 50,* 971-975.

Vietze, P., Falsey, S., Sandler, H., O'Connor, S., & Altemier, W.A. (1980). Transactional approach to prediction of child maltreatment. *Infant Mental Health Journal, 1,* 248-261.

Vitaliano, P.P., Maiuro, R.D., Bolton, P., & Armsden, G.C.(1987). A psychoepidemiologic approach to the study of disaster. *Journal of Community Psychology, 15,* 99-122.

Vostanis, P., Grattan, E., Cumella, S., & Winchester, C. (1997). Psychosocial functioning of homeless children. *Journal of the American Academy of Child and Adolescent Psychiatry, 36* (7) 881-889.

Wagner, J., & Menke, E. (1990). *The mental health of homeless children.* Paper presented at the meeting of the American Public Health Association, New York City.

Walker, L.E. (1979). *The battered woman.* New York: Harper & Row.

Walker, L.E. (1983). The battered woman syndrome study. In D. Finkelhor, R.J. Gelles, G.T. Hotaling, & M.A. Straus (Eds.), *The dark side of families: Current family violence research,* (pp. 31-48). Beverly Hills, CA: Sage.

Waters, E., & Sroufe, L.A. (1983). Social competence as a developmental construct. *Developmental Review, 3,* 79-97.

Weinraub, M., & Wolf, B. (1983). Effects of stress and social supports on mother-child interactions in single-and two-parent families. *Child Development, 54,* 1297-1311.

Weinreb, L.F., & Bassuk, E.L. (1990). Substance abuse: A growing problem among homeless families. *Family and Community Health, 13* (1), 55-64.

Weissman, M., Sholomskas, D., Pottenger, M., Prusoff, B.A., & Locke, B.Z. (1977). Assessing depressive symptoms in five psychiatric populations: A validation study. *American Journal of Epidemiology, 106,* 203-214.

Werner, E.E. (1984). Resilient children. *Young Children, 40* (1), 68-72.

Werner, E.E. (1988). Individual differences, universal needs: A 30-year study of resilient high risk infants. *Zero to Three, 8* (4), 1-5.

Werner, E.E. (1989). High-risk children in young adulthood: A longitudinal study from birth to 32 years. *American Journal of Orthopsychiatry, 59,* 72-81.

Werner, E.E., Bierman, J.M., & French, F.E. (1971). *The children of Kauai: A longitudinal study of the prenatal period to age ten.* Honolulu: University of Hawaii Press.

Werner, E.E., & Smith, R.S. (1977). *Kauai's children come of age.* Honolulu: University of Hawaii Press.

Werner, E.E., & Smith, R.S. (1982). *Vulnerable but invincible: A study of resilient children.* New York: McGraw-Hill.

Wertlieb, D., Weigel, C., Springer, T., & Feldstein, M. (1989). Temperament as a moderator of children's stressful experiences. In S. Chess, A. Thomas, & M.E. Hertz (Eds.), *Annual progress in child psychiatry and child development: 1988,* (pp. 238-254). New York: Bruner/Mazel.

Weston, D.R., Ivins, B., Zuckerman, B., Jones, C. & Lopez, R. (1989). Drug exposed babies: Research and clinical issues. *Zero to Three, 9* (5), 1-7.

Wethington, E., & Kessler, R.C. (1986). Perceived support, received support, and adjustment to stressful life events. *Journal of Health and Social Behavior, 27,* 78-89.

Whitman, B. (1987, February 24). *The crisis in homelessness: Effects on children and families.* Testimony presented before the U.S. House of Representatives Select Committee on Children, Youth, and Families. Washington, D.C.: U.S. Government Printing Office.

Whitman, B., Accardo, P., Boyert, M., & Kendagor, R. (1990). Homelessness and cognitive performance in children: A possible link. *Social Work, 35,* 516-519.

Williams, C.W. (1991). Child welfare services and homelessness: Issues in policy, philosophy, and programs. In J.H. Kryder-Coe, L.M. Salamon, & J.M. Molnar (Eds.), *Homeless children and youth,* (pp. 285-299). New Brunswick, NJ: Transactions Publishers.

Williams, T., & Kornblum, W. (1985). *Growing up poor.* Lexington, MA: Lexington Books.

Wilson, H. (1974). Parenting in poverty. *British Journal of Social Work, 4,* 241-254.

Wilson, M.N. (1986). The black extended family: An analytical consideration. *Developmental Psychology, 22,* 246-259.

Wilson, W.J., & Neckerman, K.M. (1985). Without jobs, Black men cannot support families. *Point of View, 2,* 30-35.

Wilson, W.J., & Neckerman, K.M. (1986). Poverty and family structure: The widening gap between evidence and public policy issues. In S. Danziger & D. Weinberg (Eds.), *Fighting poverty: What works and what doesn't,* (pp. 232-259). Cambridge, MA: Harvard University Press.

Winnicott, D.W. (1960). The theory of the parent-infant relationship. *International Journal of Psychoanalysis, 41,* 571-595.

Wolf, E.S. (1988). *Treating the self: Elements of clinical self psychology.* New York: Guilford.

Wolfe, D.A., Zak, L., Wilson, S., & Jaffe, P. (1986). Child witness to violence between parents: Critical issues in behavioral and social adjustment. *Journal of Abnormal Child Psychology, 14* (1), 95-104.

Wolfe, M. (1978). Childhood and privacy. In I. Altman & J.F. Wohlwill (Eds.), *Children and the environment, Vol. 3,* (pp. 175-222). New York: Plenum.

Wood, D., Valdez, R.B., Hayashi, T., & Shen, A. (1990). Homeless and housed families in Los Angeles: A study comparing demographic, economic, and family function characteristics. *American Journal of Public Health, 80,* 1049-1052.

Wright, K. (1982). Sociocultural factors in child abuse. In B.A. Bass, G.E. Wyatt, & G.J. Powell (Eds.), *The Afro-American family: Assessment, treatment, and research issues,* (pp. 237-261). New York: Grune & Stratton.

Yarrow, L.J., Rubenstein, J.L., & Pedersen, F.A. (1975). *Infant and environment. Early cognitive and emotional development.* Washington, D.C.: Hemisphere Publishing.

Zelkowitz, P. (1982). Parenting philosophies and practices. In D. Belle (Ed.), *Lives in stress: Women and depression,* (pp. 154-162). Beverly Hills, CA: Sage.

Ziesemer, C., Marcoux, L., & Marwell, B.E. (1994). Homeless children: Are they different from other low income children? *Social Work, 39* (6) 658-668.

Zigler, E., & Trickett, P.K. (1978). IQ, social competence, and evaluation of early childhood intervention programs. *American Psychologist, 33* (9), 789-798.

Zima, B.T., Wells, K.B., Benjamin, B., & Duan, N. (1996). Mental health problems among homeless mothers: Relationship to service use and child mental health problems. *Archives of General Psychiatry, 53,* 332-338.

Zima, B.T., Wells, K.B., & Freeman, H.E. (1994). Emotional and behavioral problems and severe academic delays among sheltered homeless children in Los Angeles County. *American Journal of Public Health, 84* (2) 260-264.

Zung, W.W. (1965). A Self-Rating Depression Scale. *Archives of General Psychiatry, 12,* 63-70.

Zung, W.W. (1967). Factors influencing the Self-Rating Depression Scale. *Archives of General Psychiatry, 16* (5), 543-547.

Zur-Szpiro, S., & Longfellow, C. (1982). Fathers' support to mothers and children. In D. Belle (Ed.), *Lives in stress: Women and depression*, (pp. 145-153). Beverly Hills, CA: Sage.

Index